Charlotte Mary Yonge

A Short History of England

Charlotte Mary Yonge

A Short History of England

ISBN/EAN: 9783955642587

Auflage: 1

Erscheinungsjahr: 2013

Erscheinungsort: Bremen, Deutschland

@ EHV-History in Access Verlag GmbH, Fahrenheitstr. 1, 28359 Bremen. Alle Rechte beim Verlag und bei den jeweiligen Lizenzgebern.

CONTENTS.

1. – Julius Caesar. B.C. 55. 1
2. – The Romans in Britain. A.D. 41 – 418. 4
3. – The Angle Children. A.D. 597. 7
4. – The Northmen. A.D. 858 – 958. 11
5. – The Danish Conquest. A.D. 958 – 1035. 15
6. – The Norman Conquest. A.D. 1035 – 1066. 19
7. – William the Conqueror. A.D. 1066 – 1087 22
8. – William II., Rufus. A.D. 1087 – 1100. 26
9. – Henry I., Beau-Clerc. A.D. 1100 – 1135. 29
10. – Stephen. A.D. 1135 – 1154. 32
11. – Henry II., Fitz-Empress. A.D. 1154 – 1189. 36
12. – Richard I., Lion-Heart. A.D. 1189 – 1199 40
13. – John, Lackland. A.D. 1199 – 1216. 44
14. – Henry III., of Winchester. A.D. 1216 – 1272 48
15. – Edward I., Longshanks. A.D. 1272 – 1307. 52
16. – Edward II., of Caernarvon. A.D. 1307 – 1327. 57
17. – Edward III. A.D. 1327 – 1377. 61
18. – Richard II. A.D. 1377 – 1399. 65
19. – Henry IV. A.D. 1399 – 1413. 69
20. – Henry V., of Monmouth. A.D. 1413 – 1423. 73
21. – Henry VI., of Windsor. A.D. 1423 – 1461. 77
22. – Edward IV. A.D. 1461 – 1483. 82
23. – Edward V. A.D. 1483. 86

24. – Richard III. A.D. 1483 – 1485. 90

25. – Henry VII. A.D. 1485 – 1509. 93

26. – Henry VIII. and Cardinal Wolsey.
A.D. 1509 – 1529. 97

27. – Henry VIII. and his Wives. A.D. 1528 – 1547 ... 101

28. – Edward VI. A.D. 1547 – 1553. 105

29. – Mary I. A.D. 1553 – 1558. 109

30. – Elizabeth. A.D. 1558 – 1587. 113

31. – Elizabeth (continued). A.D. 1587 – 1602. 117

32. – James I., A.D. 1602 – 1625. 121

33. – Charles I., A.D. 1625 – 1645. 125

34. – The Long Parliament. A.D. 1649. 129

35. – Death of Charles I. A.D. 1649 – 1651. 133

36. – Oliver Cromwell. A.D. 1649 – 1660. 137

37. – Charles II. A.D. 1660 – 1685. 140

38. – James II. A.D. 1685 – 1688. 144

39. – William III., and Mary II. A.D. 1689 – 1702. 148

40. – Anne. A.D. 1702 – 1714 152

41. – George I. A.D. 1714 – 1725. 156

42. – George II. A.D. 1725 – 1760. 160

43. – George III. A.D. 1760 – 1785. 164

44. – George III. (continued). A.D. 1785 – 1810. 168

45. – George III. – The Regency. A.D. 1810 – 1820. ... 172

46. – George IV. A.D. 1820-1839. 176

47. – William IV. A.D. 1830 – 1837. 180

48. – Victoria. A.D. 1837 – 1855......................................184
49. – Victoria (continued). A.D. 1855 – 1860..............188
50. – Victoria (continued). A.D. 1860 – 1872..............192

CHAPTER I.

JULIUS CAESAR. B.C. 55.

Nearly two thousand years ago there was a brave captain whose name was Julius Caesar. The soldiers he led to battle were very strong, and conquered the people wherever they went. They had no gun or gunpowder then; but they had swords and spears, and, to prevent themselves from being hurt, they had helmets or brazen caps on their heads, with long tufts of horsehair upon them, by way of ornament, and breast-plates of brass on their breasts, and on their arms they carried a sort of screen, made of strong leather. One of them carried a little brass figure of an eagle on a long pole, with a scarlet flag flying below, and wherever the eagle was seen, they all followed, and fought so bravely that nothing could long stand against them.

When Julius Caesar rode at their head, with his keen, pale hook-nosed face, and the scarlet cloak that the general always wore, they were so proud of him, and so fond of him, that there was nothing they would not do for him.

Julius Caesar heard that a little way off there was a country nobody knew anything about, except that the people were very fierce and savage, and that a sort of pearl was found in the shells of mussels which lived in the rivers. He could not bear that there should be any place that his own people, the Romans, did not know and subdue. So he commanded the ships to be prepared, and he and his soldiers embarked, watching the white cliffs on the other side of the sea grow higher and higher as he came nearer and nearer.

When he came quite up to them, he found the

savages were there in earnest. They were tall men, with long red streaming hair, and such clothes as they had were woollen, checked like plaid; but many had their arms and breasts naked, and painted all over in blue patterns. They yelled and brandished their darts, to make Julius Caesar and his Roman soldiers keep away; but he only went on to a place where the shore was not quite so steep, and there commanded his soldiers to land. The savages had run along the shore too, and there was a terrible fight; but at last the man who carried the eagle jumped down into the middle of the natives, calling out to his fellows that they must come after him, or they would lose their eagle. They all came rushing and leaping down, and thus they managed to force back the savages, and make their way to the shore.

There was not much worth having when they had made their way there. Though they came again the next year, and forced their way a good deal farther into the country, they saw chiefly bare downs, or heaths, or thick woods. The few houses were little more than piles of stones, and the people were rough and wild, and could do very little. The men hunted wild boars, and wolves and stags, and the women dug the ground, and raised a little corn, which they ground to flour between two stones to make bread; and they spun the wool of their sheep, dyed it with bright colors, and wove it into dresses. They had some strong places in the woods, with trunks of trees, cut down to shut them in from the enemy, with all their flocks and cattle; but Caesar did not get into any of these. He only made the natives give him some of their pearls, and call the Romans their masters, and then he went back to his ships, and none of the set of savages who were alive when he came saw him or his

Romans any more.

Do you know who these savages were who fought with Julius Caesar? They were called Britons. And the country he came to see? That was our very own island, England, only it was not called so then. And the place where Julius Caesar landed is called Deal, and, if you look at the map where England and France most nearly touch one another, I think you will see the name Deal, and remember it was there Julius Caesar landed, and fought with the Britons.

It was fifty-five years before our blessed Saviour was born that the Romans came. So at the top of this chapter stands B.C. (Before Christ) 55.

CHAPTER II.

THE ROMANS IN BRITAIN. A.D. 41 – 418.

It was nearly a hundred years before any more of the Romans came to Britain; but they were people who could not hear of a place without wanting to conquer it, and they never left off trying till they had done what they undertook.

One of their emperors, named Claudius, sent his soldiers to conquer the island, and then came to see it himself, and called himself Brittanicus in honor of the victory, just as if he had done it himself, instead of his generals. One British chief, whose name was Caractacus, who had fought very bravely against the Romans, was brought to Rome, with chains on his hands and feet, and set before them emperor. As he stood there, he said that, when he looked at all the grand buildings of stone and marble in the streets, he could not think why the Romans should want to take away the poor rough-stone huts of the Britons. The wife of Caractacus, who had also been brought a prisoner to Rome, fell upon her knees imploring for pity, but the conquered chief asked for nothing and exhibited no signs of fear. Claudius was kind to Caractacus; but the Romans went on conquering Britain till they had won all the part of it that lies south of the river Tweed; and, as the people beyond that point were more fierce and savage still, a very strong wall, with a bank of earth and deep ditch was made to keep them out, and always watched by Roman soldiers.

The Romans made beautiful straight roads all over the country, and they built towns. Almost all the towns whose names end in *chester* were begun by the Romans, and bits of their walls are to be seen still, built of very small bricks. Sometimes people dig up a bit of the beautiful pavement of colored tiles, in patterns, which used to be the floors of their houses, or a piece of their money, or one of their ornaments.

For the Romans held Britain for four hundred years, and tamed the wild people in the south, and taught them to speak and dress, and read and write like themselves, so that they could hardly be known from the Romans. Only the wild ones beyond the wall, and in the mountains, were as savage as ever, and, now and then, used to come and steal the cattle, and burn the houses of their neighbors who had learnt better.

Another set of wild people used to come over in boats across the North Sea and German Ocean. These people had their home in the country that is called Holstein and Jutland. They were tall men, and had blue eyes and fair hair, and they were very strong, and good-natured in a rough sort of way, though they were fierce to their enemies. There was a great deal more fighting than any one has told us about; but the end of it all was that the Roman soldiers were wanted at home, and though the great British chief we call King Arthur fought very bravely, he could not drive back the blue-eyed men in the ships; but more and more came, till, at last, they got all the country, and drove the Britons, some up into the North, some into the mountains that rise along the West of the island, and some into its west point.

The Britons used to call the blue-eyed men Saxons; but they called themselves Angles, and the country was called after them Angle-land. Don't you know what it is called now? England itself, and the people English. They spoke much the same language as we do, only more as untaught country people, and they had not so many words, because they had not so many things to see and talk about.

As to the Britons, the English went on driving them back till they only kept their mountains. There they have gone on living ever since, and talking their own old language. The English called them Welsh, a name that meant strangers, and we call them Welsh still, and their country Wales. They made a great many grand stories about their last brave chief, Arthur, till, at last, they turned into a sort of fairy tale. It was said that, when King Arthur lay badly wounded after his last battle, he bade his friend fling his sword into the river, and that then three lovely ladies came in a boat, and carried him away to a secret island. The Welsh kept on saying, for years and years, that one day king Arthur would wake up again, and give them back all Britain, which used to be their own before the English got it for themselves; but the English have had England now for thirteen hundred years, and we cannot doubt they will keep it as long as the world lasts.

It was about 400 years after our Lord was born that the Romans were going and the English coming.

CHAPTER III.

THE ANGLE CHILDREN A.D. 597.

The old English who had come to Britain were heathen, and believed in many false gods: the Sun, to whom they made Sunday sacred, as Monday was to the moon, Wednesday to a great terrible god, named Woden, and Thursday to a god named Thor, or Thunder. They thought a clap of thunder was the sound of the great hammer he carried in his hand. They thought their gods cared for people being brave, and that the souls of those who died fighting gallantly in battle were the happiest of all; but they did not care for kindness or gentleness.

Thus they often did very cruel things, and one of the worst that they did was the stealing of men, women, and children from their homes, and selling them to strangers, who made slaves of them. All England had not one king. There were generally about seven kings, each with a different part of the island and as they were often at war with one another, they used to steal one another's subjects, and sell them to merchants who came from Italy and Greece for them.

Some English children were made slaves, and carried to Rome, where they were set in the market-place to be sold. A good priest, named Gregory, was walking by. He saw their fair faces, blue eyes, and long light hair, and, stopping, he asked who they were. "Angles," he was told, "from the isle of Britain." "Angles?" he said, "they have angel faces, and they ought to be heirs with the angels in heaven." From that time this good man tried to find means to send teachers to teach the English the Christian faith. He had to wait for many years, and, in that time, he was made Pope, namely, Father-Bishop of Rome. At last he heard that one of the chief English kings, Ethelbert of Kent, had married Bertha, the daughter of the King of Paris, who was a Christian, and that she was to be allowed to bring a priest with her, and have a church to worship in.

Gregory thought this would make a beginning: so he sent a priest, whose name was Augustine, with a letter to King Ethelbert and Queen Bertha, and asked the King to listen to him. Ethelbert met Augustine in the open air, under a tree at Canterbury, and heard him tell about the true God, and JESUS CHRIST, whom He sent; and, after some time, and a great deal of teaching, Ethelbert gave up worshiping Woden and Thor, and believed in the true God, and was baptized, and many of his people with him. Then Augustine was made Archbishop of Canterbury; and, one after another, in the course of the next hundred years, all the English kingdoms learnt to know God, and broke down their idols, and became Christian.

Bishops were appointed, and churches were built, and parishes were marked off – a great many of them the very same that we have now. Here and there, when men and women wanted to be very good indeed, and to give their whole lives to doing nothing but serving God, without any of the fighting and feasting, the buying and selling of the outer world, they built houses, where they might live apart, and churches, where there might be services seven times a day. These houses were named abbeys. Those for men were, sometimes, also called monasteries, and the men in them were termed monks, while the women were called nuns, and their homes convents or nunneries. They had plain dark dresses, and hoods, and the women always had veils. The monks used to promise that they would work as well as pray, so they used to build their abbeys by some forest or marsh, and bring it all into order, turning the wild place into fields, full of wheat. Others used to copy out the Holy Scriptures and other good books upon parchment – because there was no paper in those days, nor any printing – drawing beautiful painted pictures at the beginning of the chapters, which were called illuminations. The nun did needlework and embroidery, as hangings for the altar, and garments for the priests, all bright with beautiful colors, and stiff with gold. The English nuns' work was the most beautiful to be seen anywhere.

There were schools in the abbeys, where boys were taught reading, writing, singing, and Latin, to prepare them for being clergymen; but not many others thought it needful to have anything to do with books. Even the great men thought they could farm and feast, advise the king, and consent to the laws, hunt or fight, quite as well without reading, and they did not care for much besides; for, though they were Christians, they were still rude, rough, ignorant men, who liked nothing so well as a hunt or a feast, and slept away all the evening, especially when they could get a harper to sing to them.

The English men used to wear a long dress like a carter's frock, and their legs were wound round with strips of cloth by way of stockings. Their houses were only one story, and had no chimneys – only a hole at the top for the smoke to go out at; and no glass in the windows. The only glass there was at all had been brought from Italy to put into York Cathedral, and it was thought a great wonder. So the windows had shutters to keep out the rain and wind, and the fire was in the middle of the room. At dinner-time, about twelve o'clock, the lord and lady of the house sat upon cross-legged stools, and their children and servants sat on benches; and square bits of wood called trenchers, were put before them for plates, while the servants carried round the meat on spits, and everybody cut off a piece with his own knife and at it without a fork. They drank out of cows' horns, if they had not silver cups. But though they were so rough they were often good, brave people.

CHAPTER IV.

THE NORTHMEN. A.D. 858 – 958.

There were many more of the light-haired, blue-eyed people on the further side of the North Sea who worshiped Thor and Woden still, and thought that their kindred in England had fallen from the old ways. Besides, they liked to make their fortunes by getting what they could from their neighbors. Nobody was thought brave or worthy, in Norway or Denmark, who had not made some voyages in a "long keel," as a ship was called, and fought bravely, and brought home gold cups and chains or jewels to show where he had been. Their captains were called Sea Kings, and some them went a great way, even into the Mediterranean Sea, and robbed the beautiful shores of Italy. So dreadful was it to see the fleet of long ships coming up to the shore, with a serpent for the figure-head, and a raven as the flag, and crowds of fierce warriors with axes in their hands longing for prey and bloodshed, that where we pray in church that God would deliver us from lightning and tempest, and battle and murder, our forefathers used to add, "From the fury of the Northmen, good Lord deliver us."

To England these Northmen came in great swarms, and chiefly from Denmark, so that they were generally call "the Danes." They burnt the houses, drove off the cows and sheep, killed the men, and took away the women and children to be slaves; and they were always most cruel of all where they found an Abbey with any monks or nuns, because they hated the Christian faith. By this time those seven English kingdoms I told you of had all fallen into the hands of one king. Egbert, King of the West Saxons, who reigned at Winchester, is counted as the first king of all England. His four grandsons had dreadful battles with the Danes all their lives, and the three eldest all died quite young. The youngest was the greatest and best king England ever had – Alfred the Truth-teller. As a child Alfred excited the hopes and admiration of all who saw him, and while his brothers were busy with their sports, it was his delight to kneel at his mother's knee, and recite to her the Saxon ballads which his tutor had read to him, inspiring him, at that early age, with the ardent patriotism and the passionate love of literature which rendered his character so illustrious. He was only twenty-two years old when he came to the throne, and the kingdom was overrun everywhere with the Danes. In the northern part some had even settled down and made themselves at home, as the English had done four hundred years before, and more and more kept coming in their ships: so that, though Alfred beat them in battle again and again, there was no such thing as driving them away. At last he had so very few faithful men left him, that he thought it wise to send them away, and hide himself in the Somersetshire marsh country. There is a pretty story told of him that he was hidden in the hut of a poor herdsman, whose wife, thinking he was a poor wandering soldier as he sat by the fire mending his bow and arrows, desired him to turn the cakes she had set to bake upon the hearth. Presently she found them burning, and cried out angrily, "Lazy rogue! you can't turn the cakes, though you can eat them fast enough."

However, that same spring, the brave English gained more victories; Alfred came out of his hiding place and gathered them all together, and beat the Danes, so that they asked for peace. He said he would allow those who had settled in the North of England to stay there, provided they would become Christians; and he stood godfather to their chief, and gave him the name of Ethelstane. After this, Alfred had stout ships built to meet the Danes at sea before they could come and land in England; and thus he kept them off, so that for all the rest of his reign, and that of his son and grandsons, they could do very little mischief, and for a time left off coming at all, but went to rob other countries that were not so well guarded by brave kings.

But Alfred was not only a brave warrior. He was a most good and holy man, who feared God above all things, and tried to do his very best for his people. He made good laws for them, and took care that every one should be justly treated, and that nobody should do his neighbor wrong without being punished. So many Abbeys had been burnt and the monks killed by the Danes, that there were hardly any books to be had, or scholars to read them. He invited learned men from abroad, and wrote and translated books himself for them; and he had a school in his house, where he made the young nobles learn with his own sons. He built up the churches, and gave alms to the poor; and he was always ready to hear the troubles of any poor man. Though he was always working so hard, he had a disease that used to cause him terrible pain almost every day. His last years were less peaceful than the middle ones of his reign, for the Danes tried to come again; but he beat them off by his ships at sea, and when he died at fifty-two years old, in the year 901, he left England at rest and quiet, and we always think of him as one of the greatest and best kings who ever reigned in England, or in any other country. As long as his children after him and his people went on in the good way he had taught them, all prospered with them, and no enemies hurt them; and this was all through the reigns of his son, his grandson, and great-grandsons. Their council of great men was called by a long word that is in our English, "Wise Men's Meeting," and there they settled the affairs of the kingdom. The king's wife was not called queen, but lady; and what do you think lady means? It means "loaf-giver" – giver of bread to her household and the poor. so a lady's great work is to be charitable.

CHAPTER V.

THE DANISH CONQUEST. A.D. 958 – 1035.

The last very prosperous king was Alfred's great-grandson, Edgar, who was owned as their over-lord by all the kings of the remains of the Britons in Wales and Scotland. Once, eight of these kings came to meet him at Chester, and rowed him in his barge along the river Dee. It was the grandest day a king of England enjoyed for many years. Edgar was called the peaceable, because there were no attacks by the Danes at all through his reign. In fact, the Northmen and Danes had been fighting among themselves at home, and these fights generally ended in some one going off as a Sea-King, with all his friends, and trying to gain a new home in some fresh country. One great party of Northmen under a very tall and mighty chief named Rollo, had some time before, thus gone to France, and forced the King to give them a great piece of his country, just opposite to England, which was called after them Normandy. There they learned to talk French, and grew like Frenchmen, though they remained a great deal braver, and more spirited than any of their neighbors.

There were continually fleets of Danish ships coming to England; and the son of Edgar, whose name was Ethelred, was a helpless, cowardly sort of man, so slow and tardy, that his people called him Ethelred the Unready. Instead of fitting out ships to fight against the Danes, he took the money the ships ought to have cost to pay them to go away without plundering; and as to those who had come into the country without his leave, he called them his guard, took them into his pay, and let them live in the houses of the English, where they were very rude, and gave themselves great airs, making the English feed them on all their best meat, and bread, and beer, and always call them Lord Danes. He made friends himself with the Northmen, or Normans, who had settled in France, and married Emma, the daughter of their duke; but none of his plans prospered: things grew worse and worse, and his mind and his people's grew so bitter against the Danes, that at last it was agreed that all over the South of England every Englishman should rise up in one night and murder the Dane who lodged in his house.

Among those Danes who were thus wickedly killed was the sister of the King of Denmark. Of course he was furious when he heard of it, and came over to England determined to punish the cruel, treacherous king and people, and take the whole island for his own. He did punish the people, killing, burning, and plundering wherever he went; but he could never get the king into his hands, for Ethelred went off in the height of the danger to Normandy, where he had before sent his wife Emma, and her children, leaving his eldest son(child of his first wife), Edmund Ironside, to fight for the kingdom as best he might.

The King of Denmark died in the midst of his English war; but his son Cnut went on with the conquest he had begun, and before long Ethelred, the Unready died, and Edmund Ironside was murdered, and Cnut became King of England, as well as of Denmark. He became a Christian, and married Emma, Ethelred's widow, though she was much older than himself. He had been a hard and cruel man, but he now laid aside his evil ways, and became a noble and wise and just king, a lover of churches and good men;

and the English seem to have been as well off under him as if he had been one of their own kings. There is no king of whom more pleasant stories are told. One is of his wanting to go to church at Ely Abbey one cold Candlemas Day. Ely was on a hill in the middle of a great marsh. The marsh was frozen over; not strong enough to bear, and they all stood looking at it. Then out stepped a stout countryman, who was so fat, that his nickname was The Pudding. "Are you all afraid?" he said. "I will go over at once before the king." "Will you," said the king, "then I will come after you, for whatever bears you will bear me." Cnut was a little, slight man, and he got easily over, and Pudding got a piece of land for his reward.

These servants of the king used to flatter him. They told him he was lord of land and sea, and that every thing would obey him. "Let us try," said Cnut, who wished to show them how foolish and profane they were; "bring out my chair to the sea-side." He was at Southampton at the time, close to the sea, and the tide was coming in. "Now sea," he said, as he sat down, "I am thy lord, dare not to come near, nor wet my feet." Of course the waves rolled on, and splashed over him; and he turned to his servants, and bade them never say words that took away from the honor due to the only Lord of heaven and earth. He never put on his crown again after this, but hung it up in Winchester Cathedral. He was a thorough good king, and there was much grief when he died, stranger though he was.

A great many Danes had made their homes in Yorkshire and Lincolnshire, ever since Alfred's time, and some of their customs are still left there, and some of their words. The worst of them was that they were great drunkards, and the English learnt this bad custom of them.

CHAPTER VI.

THE NORMAN CONQUEST. A.D. 1035 – 1066.

Cnut left three sons; but one was content to be only King of Denmark, and the other two died very soon. So a great English nobleman, called Earl Godwin, set up as king, Edward, one of those sons of Ethelred the Unready who had been sent away to Normandy. He was a very kind, good, pious man, who loved to do good. He began the building of our grand church at Westminster Abbey, and he was so holy that he was called the Confessor, which is a word for good men not great enough to be called saints. He was too good-natured, as you will say when you hear that one day, when he was in bed, he saw a thief come cautiously into his room, open the chest where his treasure was, and take out the money- bags. Instead of calling anyone, or seizing the man, the king only said, sleepily, "Take care, you rogue, or my chancellor will catch you and give you a good whipping."

You can fancy that nobody much minded such a king as this, and so there were many disturbances in his time. Some of them rose out of the king – who had been brought up in Normandy – liking the Normans better than the English. They really were much cleverer and more sensible, for they had learnt a great deal in France, while the English had forgotten much of what Alfred and his sons had taught them, and all through the long, sad reign of Ethelred had been getting more dull, and clumsy and rude. Moreover, they had learnt of the Danes to be sad drunkards; but both they and the Danes thought the Norman French fine gentlemen, and could not bear the sight of them.

Think, then, how angry they all were when it began to be said that King Edward wanted to leave his kingdom of England to his mother's Norman nephew, Duke William, because all his own near relations were still little boys, not likely to be grown up by the time the old king died. Many of the English wished for Harold, the son of Earl Godwin, a brave, spirited man; but Edward sent him to Normandy, and there Duke William made him swear an oath not to do anything to hinder the kingdom from being given to Duke William.

Old King Edward died soon after, and Harold said at once that his promise had been forced and cheated from him, so that he need not keep it, and he was crowned King of England. This filled William with anger. He called all his fighting Normans together, fitted out ships, and sailed across the English Channel to Dover. The figure-head of his own ship was a likeness of his second little boy, named William. He landed at Pevensey, in Sussex, and set up his camp while Harold was away in the North, fighting with a runaway brother of his own, who had brought the Norwegians to attack Yorkshire. Harold had just won a great battle over these enemies when he heard that William and his Normans had landed, and he had to hurry the whole length of England to meet them.

Many of the English would not join him, because they did not want him for their king. But though his army was not large, it was very brave. When he reached Sussex, he placed all his men on the top of a low hill, near Hastings, and caused them to make a fence all round, with a ditch before it, and in the middle was his own standard, with a fighting man embroidered upon it. Then the Normans rode up on their war-horses to attack him, one brave knight going first, singing. The war-horses stumbled in the ditch, and the long spears of the English killed both men and horses. Then William ordered his archers to shoot their arrows high in the air. They came down like hail into the faces and on the heads of the English. Harold himself was pierced by one in the eye. The Normans charged the fence again, and broke through; and, by the time night came on, Harold himself and all his brave Englishmen were dead. They did not flee away; they all staid, and were killed, fighting to the last; and only then was Harold's standard of the fighting man rooted up, and William's standard – a cross, which had been blessed by the Pope – planted instead of it. So ended the battle of Hastings, in the year 1066.

The land has had a great many "conquests" hitherto – the Roman conquest, the English conquest, and now the Norman conquest. But there have been no more since; and the kings and queens have gone on in one long line ever since, from William of Normandy down to Queen Victoria.

CHAPTER VII.

WILLIAM THE CONQUEROR. A.D. 1066 – 1087.

The king who had conquered England was a brave, strong man, who had been used to fighting and struggling ever since he was a young child.

He really feared God, and was in many ways a good man; but it had not been right of him to come and take another people's country by force; and the having done one wrong thing often makes people grow worse and worse. Many of the English were unwilling to have William as their king, and his Norman friends were angry that he would not let them have more of the English lands, nor break the English laws. So they were often rising up against him; and each time he had to put them down he grew more harsh and stern. He did not want to be cruel; but he did many cruel things, because it was the only way to keep England.

When the people of Northumberland rose against him, and tried to get back the old set of kings, he had the whole country wasted with fire and sword, till hardly a town or village was left standing. He did this to punish the Northumbrians, and frighten the rest. But he did another thing that was worse, because it was only for his own amusement. In Hampshire, near his castle of Winchester, there was a great space of heathy ground, and holly copse and beeches and oaks above it, with deer and boars running wild in the glades – a beautiful place for hunting, only that there were so many villages in it that the creatures were disturbed and killed. William liked hunting more than anything else – his people said he loved the high deer as if he was their father, – and to keep the place clear for them, he turned out all the inhabitants, and pulled down their houses, and made laws against any one killing his game. The place he thus cleared is still called the New Forest, though it is a thousand years old.

An old Norman law that the English grumbled about very much was, that as soon as a bell was rung, at eight o'clock every evening, everyone was to put out candle and fire, and go to bed. The bell was called the curfew, and many old churches ring it still.

William caused a great list to be made of all the lands in the country, and who held them. We have this list still, and it is called Domesday Book. It shows that a great deal had been taken from the English and given to the Normans. The king built castles, with immensely thick, strong walls, and loop-hole windows, whence to shoot arrows; and here he placed his Normans to keep the English down. But the Normans were even more unruly than the English, and only his strong hand kept them in order. They rode about in armor – helmets on their heads, a shirt of mail, made of iron linked together, over their bodies, gloves and boots of iron, swords by their sides, and lances in their hands – and thus they could bear down all before them. They called themselves knights, and were always made to take an oath to befriend the weak, and poor, and helpless; but they did not often keep it towards the poor English.

William had four sons – Robert, who was called Court-hose or Short-legs; William, called Rufus, because he had red hair; Henry, called Beau- clerc or the fine scholar; and Richard, who was still a lad when he was killed by a stag in the New Forest.

Robert, the eldest, was a wild, rude, thoughtless youth; but he fancied himself fit to govern Normandy, and asked his father to give it up to him. King William answered, "I never take my clothes off before I go to bed," meaning that Robert must wait for his death. Robert could not bear to be laughed at, and was very angry. Soon after, when he was in the castle court, his two brothers, William and Henry, grew riotous, and poured water down from the upper windows on him and his friends. He flew into a passion, dashed upstairs with his sword in his hand, and might have killed his brothers if their father had not come in to protect them. Then he threw himself on his horse and galloped away, persuaded some friends to join him, and actually fought a battle with his own father, in which the old king was thrown off his horse, and hurt in the hand; but we must do the prince the justice to say that when he recognized his father in the knight whom he had unseated, he was filled with grief and horror, and eagerly sought his pardon, and tenderly raised him from the ground. Then Robert wandered about, living on money that his mother, Queen Matilda, sent him, though his father was angry with her for doing so, and this made the first quarrel the husband and wife had ever had.

Not long after, William went to war with the King of France. He had caused a city to be burnt down, and was riding through the ruins, when his horse trod on some hot ashes, and began to plunge. The king was thrown forward on the saddle, and, being a very heavy, stout man, was so much hurt, that, after a few weeks, in the year 1087, he died at a little monastery, a short way from Rouen, the chief city of his dukedom of Normandy.

He was the greatest man of his time, and he had much good in him; and when he lay on his death-bed he grieved much for all the evil he had brought upon the English; but that could not undo it. He had been a great church-builder, and so were his Norman bishops and barons. You always know their work, because it has round pillars, and round arches, with broad borders of zig-zags, and all manner of patterns round them.

In the end, the coming of the Normans did the English much good, by brightening them up and making them less dull and heavy; but they did not like having a king and court who talked French, and cared more for Normandy than for England.

CHAPTER VIII.

WILLIAM II., RUFUS. A.D. 1087-1100.

William the Conqueror was obliged to let Normandy fall to Robert, his eldest son; but he thought he could do as he pleased about England, which he had won for himself. He had sent off his second son, William, to England, with his ring to Westminster, giving him a message that he hoped the English people would have him for their king. And they did take him, though they would hardly have done do if they had known what he would be like when he was left to himself. But while he was kept under by his father, they only knew that he had red hair and a ruddy face, and had more sense than his brother Robert. He is sometimes called the Red King, but more commonly William Rufus. Things went worse than ever with the poor English in his time; for at lest William the Conqueror had made everybody mind the law, but now William Rufus let his cruel soldiers do just as they pleased, and spoil what they did not want. It was of no use to complain, for the king would only laugh and make jokes. He did not care for God or man; only for being powerful, for feasting, and for hunting.

Just at this time there was a great stir in Europe. Jerusalem – that holy city, where our blessed Lord had taught, where he had been crucified, and where he had risen from the dead – was a place where everyone wished to go and worship, and this they called going on pilgrimage. A beautiful church had once been built over the sepulchre where our Lord had lain, and enriched with gifts. But for a long time past Jerusalem had been in the hands of an Eastern people, who think their false prophet, Mahommed, greater than our blessed Lord. These Mahommedans used to rob and ill-treat the pilgrims, and make them pay great sums of money for leave to come into Jerusalem. At last a pilgrim, named Peter the Hermit, came home, and got leave from the Pope to try to go to the Holy Land, and fight to get the Holy Sepulchre back into Christian hands again. He used to preach in the open air, and the people who heard him were so stirred up that they all shouted out, "It is God's will! It is God's will!" And each who undertook to go and fight in the East received a cross cut out into cloth, red or white, to wear on his shoulder. Many thousands promised to go on this crusade, as they called it, among them was Robert, Duke of Normandy. But he had wasted his money, so that he could not fit out an army to take with him. So he offered to give up Normandy to his brother William while he was gone, if William would let him have the money he wanted. The Red King was very ready to make such a bargain, and he laughed at the Crusaders, and thought that they were wasting their time and trouble.

They had a very good man to lead them, named Godfrey de Buillon; and, after many toils and troubles, they did gain Jerusalem, and could kneel, weeping, at the Holy Sepulchre. It was proposed to make Robert King of Jerusalem, but he would not accept the offer, and Godfrey was made king instead, and staid to guard the holy places, while Duke Robert set out on his return home.

In the meantime, the Red King had gone on in as fierce and ungodly a way as ever, laughing good advice to scorn, and driving away the good Archbishop of Canterbury, St. Anselm, and everyone else who tried to warn him or withstand his wickedness. One day, in the year 1100, he went out to hunt deer in the New Forest, which his father had wasted, laughing and jesting in his rough way. By and by he was found under an oak tree, with an arrow through his heart; and a wood-cutter took up his body in his cart, and carried it to Winchester Cathedral, where is was buried.

Who shot the arrow nobody knew, and nobody ever will know. Some thought it must be a knight, named Walter Tyrrell, to whom the king had given three long good arrows that morning. He rode straight away to Southampton, and went off to the Holy Land; so it is likely that he knew something about the king's death. But he never seems to have told any one, whether it was only an accident, or a murder, or who did it. Anyway, it was a fearful end, for a bad man to die in his sin, without a moment to repent and pray.

CHAPTER IX.

HENRY I., BEAU-CLERC. A.D. 1100 – 1135.

Henry, the brother of William Rufus, was one of the hunting party; and as soon as the cry spread through the forest that the king was dead, he rode off at full speed to Winchester, and took possession of all his brother's treasure. William Rufus had never been married, and left no children, and Henry was much the least violent and most sensible of the brothers; and, as he promised to govern according to the old laws of England, he did not find it difficult to persuade the people to let him be crowned king.

He was not really a good man, and he could be very cruel sometimes, as well as false and cunning; but he kept good order, and would not allow such horrible things to be done as in his brother's time. So the English were better off than they had been, and used to say the king would let no one break the laws but himself. They were pleased, too, that Henry married a lady who was half English – Maude, the daughter of Malcolm Greathead, King of Scotland, and of a lady of the old English royal line. They loved her greatly, and called her good Queen Maude.

Robert came back to Normandy, and tried to make himself King of England; but Henry soon drove him back. The brothers went on quarreling for some years, and Robert managed Normandy miserably, and wasted his money, so that he sometimes had no clothes to wear, and lay in bed for want of them.

Some of the Normans could not bear this any longer, and invited Henry to come and take the dukedom. He came with an army, many of whom were

English, and fought a battle with Robert and his faithful Normans at Trenchebray, in Normandy. They gained a great victory, and the English thought it made up for Hastings. Poor Robert was made prisoner by his brother, who sent him off to Cardiff Castle, in Wales, where he lived for twenty-eight years, and then died, and was buried in Gloucester Cathedral, with his figure made in bog oak over his monument.

Henry had two children – William and Maude. The girl was married to the Emperor of Germany and the boy was to be the husband of Alice, daughter to the Count of Anjou, a great French Prince, whose lands were near Normandy. It was the custom to marry children very young then, before they were old enough to leave their parents and make a home for themselves. So William was taken by his father to Anjou, and there married to the little girl, and then she was left behind, while he was to return to England with his father. Just as he was going to embark, a man came to the king, and begged to have the honor of taking him across in his new vessel, called the White Ship. Henry could not change his own plans; but, as the man begged so hard, he said his son, the young bridegroom, and his friends might go in the White Ship. They sailed in the evening, and there was a great merry-making on board, till the sailors grew so drunk that they did not know how to guide the ship, and ran her against a rock. She filled with water and began to sink. A boat was lowered, and William safely placed in it; but, just as he was rowed off he heard the cries of the ladies who were left behind, and caused the oarsmen to turn back for them. So many drowning wretches crowded into it, as soon as it came near, that it sank with their weight, and all were lost. Only the top-mast of the ship remained above water, and to it clung a butcher and the owner of the ship all night long. When daylight came, and the owner knew that the king's son was really dead, and by his fault, he lost heart, let go the mast and was drowned. Only the butcher was taken off alive; and for a long time no one durst tell the king what had happened. At last a boy was sent to fall at his feet, and tell him his son was dead. He was a broken-hearted man, and never knew gladness again all the rest of his life.

His daughter Maude had lost her German husband, and came home. He made her marry Geoffrey of Anjou, the brother of his son's wife, and called upon all his chief noblemen to swear that they would take her for their queen in England and their duchess in Normandy after his own death.

He did not live much longer. His death was caused, in the year 1135, by eating too much of the fish called lamprey, and he was buried in Reading Abbey.

CHAPTER X.

STEPHEN. A.D. 1135 – 1154.

Neither English nor Normans had ever been ruled by a woman, and the Empress Maude, as she still called herself, was a proud, disagreeable, ill-tempered woman, whom nobody liked. So her cousin, Stephen de Blois – whose mother, Adela, had been daughter of William the Conqueror – thought to obtain the crown of England by promising to give everyone what they wished. It was very wrong of him; for he, like all the other barons, had sworn that Maude should reign. But the people knew he was a kindly, gracious sort of person, and greatly preferred him to her. So he was crowned; and at once all the Norman barons, whom King Henry had kept down, began to think they could have their own way. They built strong castles, and hired men, with whom they made war upon each other, robbed one another's tenants, and, when they saw a peaceable traveler on his way, they would dash down upon him, drag him into the castle, take away all the jewels or money he had about him, or, if he had none, they would shut him up and torment him till he could get his friends to pay them a sum to let him loose.

Stephen, who was a kind-hearted man himself, tried to stop these cruelties; but then the barons turned round on him, told him he was not their proper king, and invited Maude to come and be crowned in his stead. She came very willingly; and her uncle, King David of Scotland, set out with an army to fight for her; but all the English in the north came out to drive him back; and they beat him and his Scots at what they call the Battle of the Standard, because the cause the English had a holy standard, which was kept in Durham Cathedral. Soon after, Stephen was taken prisoner at a battle at Lincoln, and there was nothing to prevent Maude from being queen but her own bad temper. She went to Winchester, and was there proclaimed; but she would not speak kindly or gently to the people; and when her friends entreated her to reply more kindly, she flew into a passion, and it is even said that she gave a box on the ear to her uncle – the good King of Scotland, who had come to help her – for reproving her for her harsh answers. When Stephen's wife came to beg her to set him free, promising that he should go away beyond the seas, and never interfere with her again, she would not listen, and drove her away. But she soon found how foolish she had been. Stephen's friends would have been willing that he should give up trying to be king, but they could not leave him in prison for life; and so they went on fighting for him, while more and more of the English joined them, as they felt how bad and unkind a queen they had in the Empress. Indeed, she was so proud and violent, that her husband would not come over to England to help her, but staid to govern Normandy. She was soon in great distress, and had to flee from Winchester, riding through the midst of the enemy, and losing almost all her friends by the way as they were slain or made prisoners. Her best helper of all – Earl Robert of Gloucester – was taken while guarding her; and she could only get to his town of Gloucester by lying down in a coffin, with holes for air, and being thus carried through all the country, where she had made everyone hate her.

Stephen's wife offered to set the Earl free, if the other side would release her husband; and this exchange was brought about. Robert then went to Normandy, to fetch Maude's little son Henry, who was ten years old, leaving her, as he thought, safe in Oxford Castle; but no sooner was he gone than Stephen brought his army, and besieged the Castle – that is, he brought his men round it, tried to climb up the walls, or beat them down with heavy beams, and hindered any food from being brought in. Everything in the castle that could be eaten was gone; but Maude was determined not to fall into her enemy's hands. It was the depth of winter; the river below the walls was frozen over, and snow was on the ground. One night, Maude dressed herself and three of her knights all in white, and they were, one by one, let down by ropes from the walls. No one saw them in the snow. They crossed the river on the ice, walked a great part of the night, and at last came to Abingdon, where horses were waiting for them, and thence they rode to Wallingford, where Maude met her little son.

There was not much more fighting after this. Stephen kept all the eastern part of the kingdom, and Henry was brought up at Gloucester till his father sent for him, to take leave of him before going on a crusade. Geoffrey died during this crusade. He was fond of hunting, and was generally seen with a spray of broom blossom in his cap. The French name for this plant is *genet*; and thus his nickname was "Plantagenet;" and this became a kind of surname to the kings of England.

Henry, called Fitz-empress – or "the Empress's son" – came to England again as soon as he was grown up; but instead of going to war, he made an agreement with Stephen. Henry would not attack Stephen any more, but leave him to reign all the days of his life, provided Stephen engaged that Henry should reign instead of his own son after his death. This made Stephen's son, Eustace, very angry, and he went away in a rage to raise troops to maintain his cause; but he died suddenly in the midst of his wild doings, and the king, his father, did not live long after him, but died in 1154.

Maude had learnt wisdom by her misfortunes. She had no further desire to be queen, but lived a retired life in a convent, and was much more respected there than as queen.

CHAPTER XI.

HENRY II., FITZ-EMPRESS. A.D. 1154-1189.

Henry Fitz-Empress is counted as the first king of the Plantagenet family, also called the House of Anjou. He was a very clever, brisk, spirited man, who hardly ever sat down, but was always going from place to place, and who would let no one disobey him. He kept everybody in order, pulled down almost all the Castles that had been built in Stephen's time, and would not let the barons ill-treat the people. Indeed, everyone had been so mixed up together during the wars in Stephen's reign, that the grandchildren of the Normans who had come over with William the Conqueror were now quite English in their feelings. French was, however, chiefly spoken at court. The king was really a Frenchman, and he married a French wife Eleanor, the lady of Aquitaine, a great dukedom in the South of France; and, as Henry had already Normandy and Anjou, he really was lord of nearly half France. He ruled England well; but he was not a good man, for he cared for power and pleasure more than for what was right; and sometimes he fell into such rages that he would roll on the floor, and bite the rushes and sticks it was strewn with. He made many laws. One was that, if a priest or monk was thought to have committed any crime, he should be tried by the king's judge, instead of the bishop. The Archbishop of Canterbury, Thomas a Becket, did not think it right to consent to this law; and, though he and the king had once been great friends, Henry was so angry with him that he was forced to leave England, and take shelter with the King of France. Six years passed by, and the king pretended to be reconciled to him, but still, when they met, would not give him the kiss of peace. The archbishop knew that this showed that the king still hated him; but his flock had been so long without a shepherd that he thought it his duty to go back to them. Just after his return, he laid under censure some persons who had given offence. They went and complained to the king, and Henry exclaimed in passion, "Will no one rid me of this turbulent priest?" Four of his knights who heard these words set forth to Canterbury. The archbishop guessed why they were come; but he would not flee again, and waited for them by the altar in the cathedral, not even letting the doors be shut. There they slew him; and thither, in great grief at the effect of his own words, the king came – three years later – to show his penitence by entering barefoot, kneeling before Thomas's tomb, and causing every priest or monk in turn to strike him with a rod. We should not exactly call Thomas a martyr now, but he was thought so then, because he died for upholding the privileges of the Church, and he was held to be a very great saint.

While this dispute was going on, the Earl of Pembroke, called Strongbow, one of Henry's nobles, had gone over to Ireland and obtained a little kingdom there, which he professed to hold of Henry; and thus the Kings of England became Lords of Ireland, though for a long time they only had the Province of Leinster, and were always at war with the Irish around.

Henry was a most powerful king; but his latter years were very unhappy. His wife was not a good woman, and her sons were all disobedient and rebellious. Once all the three eldest, Henry, Richard, and Geoffrey, and their mother, ran away together from his court, and began to make war upon him. He was much stronger and wiser than they so he soon forced them to submit; and he sent Queen Eleanor away, and shut her up in a strong castle in England as long as he lived. Here sons were much more fond of her than of their father, and they thought this usage so hard, that they were all the more ready to break out against him. The eldest son, Henry, was leading an army against his father, when he was taken ill, and felt himself dying. He sent an entreaty that his father would forgive him, and come to see him; but the young man had so often been false and treacherous, that Henry feared it was only a trick to get him as a prisoner, and only sent his ring and a message of pardon; and young Henry died, pressing the ring to his lips, and longing to hear his father's voice.

Geoffrey, the third son, was killed by a fall from his horse, and there were only two left alive, Richard and John. Just at this time, news came that the Mahommedans in the Holy Land had won Jerusalem back again; and the Pope called on all Christian princes to leave off quarreling, and go on a crusade to recover the Holy Sepulchre.

The kings of England and France, young Richard, and many more, were roused to take the cross; but while arrangements for going were being made, a fresh dispute about them arose, and Richard went away in a rage, got his friends together, and, with King Philip of France to help him, began to make war. His father was feeble, and worn out, and could not resist as in former times. He fell ill, and gave up the struggle, saying he would grant all they asked. The list of Richard's friends whom he was to pardon was brought to him, and the first name he saw in it was that of John, his youngest son, and his darling, the one who had never before rebelled. That quite broke his heart, his illness grew worse, and he talked about an old eagle being torn to pieces by his eaglets. And so, in the year 1189, Henry II. died the saddest death, perhaps, that an old man can die, for his sons had brought down his gray hairs with sorrow to the grave.

CHAPTER XII.

RICHARD I., LION-HEART A.D. 1189 – 1199.

Richard was greatly grieved at his father's death, and when he came and looked at the dead body, in Fontevraud Abbey Church, he cried out, "Alas! it was I who killed him!" But it was too late now: he could not make up for what he had done, and he had to think about the Crusade he had promised to make. Richard was so brave and strong that he was called Lion-heart; he was very noble and good in some ways, but his fierce, passionate temper did him a great deal of harm. He, and King Philip of France, and several other great princes, all met in the island of Sicily in the Mediterranean Sea, and thence sailed for the Holy Land. The lady whom Richard was to marry came to meet him in Sicily. Her name was Berengaria; but, as it was Lent, he did not marry her then. She went on to the Holy Land in a ship with his sister Joan, and tried to land in the island of Cypress; but the people were inhospitable, and would not let them come. So Richard, in his great anger, conquered the isle, and was married to Berengaria there.

The Mahommedans who held Palestine at that time were called Saracens, and had a very brave prince at their head named Saladin, which means Splendor of Religion. He was very good, just, upright, and truth- telling, and his Saracens fought so well, that the Crusaders would hardly have won a bit of ground if the Lion-heart had not been so brave. At last, they did take one city on the coast named Acre; and one of the princes, Leopold, Duke of Austria, set up his banner on the walls. Richard did not think it ought to be there: he pulled it up and threw it down into the ditch, asking the duke how he durst take the honors of a king. Leopold was sullen, and brooded over the insult, and King Philip thought Richard so overbearing, that he could not bear to be in the army with him any longer. In truth, though Philip had pretended to be his friend, and had taken his part against his father, that was really only to hurt King Henry; he hated Richard quite as much, or more, and only wanted to get home first in order to do him as much harm as he could while he was away. So Philip said it was too hot for him in the Holy Land, and made him ill. He sailed back to France, while Richard remained, though the climate really did hurt his health, and he often had fevers there. When he was ill, Saladin used to send him grapes, and do all he could to show how highly he thought of so brave a man. Once Saladin sent him a beautiful horse; Richard told the Earl of Salisbury to try it, and no sooner was the earl mounted, than the horse ran away with him to the Saracen army. Saladin was very much vexed, and was afraid it would be taken for a trick to take the English king prisoner, and he gave the earl a quieter horse to ride back with. Richard fought one terrible battle at Joppa with the Saracens, and then he tried to go on to take Jerusalem; but he wanted to leave a good strong castle behind him at Ascalon, and set all his men to work to build it up. When they grumbled, he worked with them, and asked the duke to do the same; but Leopold said gruffly that he was not a carpenter or a mason. Richard was so provoked that he struck him a blow, and the duke went home in a rage.

So many men had gone home, that Richard found his army was not strong enough to try to take Jerusalem. He was greatly grieved, for he knew it was his own fault for not having shown the temper of a

Crusader; and when he came to the top of a hill whence the Holy City could be seen, he would not look at it, but turned away, saying, "They who are not worthy to win it are not worthy to behold it." It was of no use for him to stay with so few men; besides, tidings came from home that King Philip and his own brother, John, were doing all the mischief they could. So he made a peace for three years between the Saracens and Christians, hoping to come back again after that to rescue Jerusalem. But on his way home there were terrible storms; his ships were scattered, and his own ship was driven up into the Adriatic Sea, where he was robbed by pirates, or sea robbers, and then was shipwrecked. There was no way for him to get home but through the lands of Leopold of Austria; so he pretended to be a merchant, and set out attended only by a boy. He fell ill at a little inn, and while he was in bed the boy went into the kitchen with the king's glove in his belt. It was an embroidered glove, such as merchants never used, and people asked questions, and guessed that the boy's master must be some great man. The Duke of Austria heard of it, sent soldiers to take him, and shut him up as a prisoner in one of his castles. Afterwards, the duke gave him up for a large sum of money to the Emperor of Germany. All this time Richard's wife and mother had been in great sorrow and fear, trying to find out what had become of him. It is said that he was found at last by his friend, the minstrel Blondel. A minstrel was a person who made verses and sang them. Many of the nobles and knights in Queen Eleanor's Duchy of Aquitaine were minstrels – and Richard was a very good one himself, and amused himself in his captivity by making verses. This is certainly true – though I cannot answer for it that the pretty story is true, which says that Blondel sung at all the castle courts in Germany, till he heard his master's voice take up and reply to his song.

The Queens, Eleanor and Berengaria, raised a ransom – that is, a sum of money to buy his freedom – though his brother John tried to prevent them, and the King of France did his best to hinder the emperor from releasing him; but the Pope insisted that the brave crusader should be set at liberty: and Richard came home, after a year and a half of captivity. He freely forgave John for all the mischief he had done or tried to do, though he thought so ill of him as to say, "I wish I may forget John's injuries to me as soon as he will forget my pardon of him."

Richard only lived two years after he came back. He was besieging a castle in Aquitaine, where there was some treasure that he thought was unlawfully kept from him, when he was struck in the shoulder by a bolt from a cross-bow, and the surgeons treated it so unskilfully that in a few days he died. The man who had shot the bolt was made prisoner, but the Lionheart's last act was to command that no harm should be done to him. The soldiers, however, in their grief and rage for the king, did put him to death in a cruel manner.

Richard desired to be burned at the feet of his father, in Fontevraud Abbey, where he once bewailed his undutiful conduct, and now wished his body forever to lie in penitence. The figures in stone, of the father, mother, and son, who quarreled so much in life, all lie on one monument now, and with them Richard's youngest sister Joan, who died nearly at the same time as he died, party of grief for him.

CHAPTER XIII.

JOHN, LACKLAND. A.D. 1199 – 1216.

As a kind of joke, John, King Henry's youngest son, had been called Lackland, because he had nothing when his brothers each had some great dukedom. The name suited him only too well before the end of his life. The English made him king at once. They always did take a grown-up man for their king, if the last king's son was but a child. Richard had never had any children, but his brother Geoffrey, who was older than John, had left a son named Arthur, who was about twelve years old, and who was rightly the Duke of Normandy and Count of Anjou. King Philip, who was always glad to vex whoever was king of England, took Arthur under his protection, and promised to get Normandy out of John's hands. However, John had a meeting with him and persuaded him to desert Arthur, and marry his son Louis to John's own niece, Blanche, who had a chance of being queen of part of Spain. Still Arthur lived at the French King's court, and when he was sixteen years old, Philip helped him to raise an army and go to try his fortune against his uncle. He laid siege to Mirabeau, a town where his grandmother, Queen Eleanor, was living. John, who was then in Normandy, hurried to her rescue, beat Arthur's army, made him prisoner and carried him off, first to Rouen, and then to the strong castle of Falaise. Nobody quite knows what was done to him there. The governor, Hubert de Burgh, once found him fighting hard, though with no weapon but a stool, to defend himself from some ruffians who had been sent to put out his eyes. Hubert saved him from these men, but shortly after this good man was sent elsewhere by the king, and John came himself to

Falaise. Arthur was never seen alive again, and it is believed that John took him out in a boat in the river at night, stabbed him with his own hand, and threw his body into the river. There was, any way, no doubt that John was guilty of his nephew's death, and he was fully known to be one of the most selfish and cruel men who ever lived; and so lazy, that he let Philip take Normandy from him, without stirring a finger to save the grand old dukedom of his forefathers; so that nothing is left of it to us now but the four little islands, Guernsey, Jersey, Alderney, and Sark.

Matters became much worse in England, when he quarreled with the Pope, whose name was Innocent, about who should be archbishop of Canterbury. The Pope wanted a man named Stephen Langton to be archbishop, but the king swore he should never come into the kingdom. Then the Pope punished the kingdom, by forbidding all church services in all parish churches. The was termed putting the kingdom under an interdict. John was not much distressed by this, though his people were; but when he found that Innocent was stirring up the King of France to come to attack him, he thought it time to make his peace with the Pope. So he not only consented to receive Stephen Langton, but he even knelt down before the Pope's legate, or messenger, and took off his crown, giving it up to the legate, in token that he only held the kingdom from the Pope. It was two or three days before it was given back to him; and the Pope held himself to be lord of England, and made the king and people pay him money whenever he demanded it.

All this time John's cruelty and savageness were making the whole kingdom miserable; and at last the great barons could bear it no longer. They met together and agreed that they would make John swear to govern by the good old English laws that had prevailed before the Normans came. The difficulty was to be sure of what these laws were, for most of the copies of them had been lost. However, Archbishop Langton and some of the wisest of the barons put together a set of laws – some copied, some recollected, some old, some new – but all such as to give the barons some control of the king, and hinder him from getting savage soldiers together to frighten people into doing whatever he chose to make them. These laws they called Magna Carta, or the great charter; and they all came in armor, and took John by surprise at Windsor. He came to meet them in a meadow named Runnymede, on the bank of the Thames, and there they forced him to sign the charter, for which all Englishmen are grateful to them.

But he did not mean to keep it! No, not he! He had one of his father's fits of rage when he got back to Windsor Castle – he gnawed the sticks for rage and swore he was no king. Then he sent for more of the fierce soldiers, who went about in bands, ready to be hired, and prepared to take vengeance on the barons. They found themselves not strong enough to make head against him; so they invited Louis, the son of Philip of France and husband of John's niece, to come and be their king. He came, and was received in London, while John and his bands of soldiers were roaming about the eastern counties, wasting and burning everywhere till they came to the Wash – that curious bay between Lincolnshire and Norfolk, where so many rivers run into the sea. There is a safe way across the sands in this bay when the tide is low, but when it is coming in and meets the rivers, the waters rise suddenly into a flood. So it happened to King John; he did get out himself, but all carts with his goods and treasures were lost, and many of his men. He was full of rage and grief, but he went on to the abbey where he meant to sleep. He supped on peaches and new ale, and soon after became very ill. He died in a few days, a miserable, disgraced man, with half his people fighting against him and London in the hands of his worst enemy.

CHAPTER XIV.

HENRY III., OF WINCHESTER. A.D. 1216 – 1272.

King John left two little sons, Henry and Richard, nine and seven years old, and all the English barons felt that they would rather have Henry as their king than the French Louis, whom they had only called in because John was such a wretch. So when little Henry had been crowned at Gloucester, with his mother's bracelet, swearing to rule according to Magna Carta, and good Hubert de Burgh undertook to govern for him, one baron after another came back to him. Louis was beaten in a battle at Lincoln; and when his wife sent him more troops, Hubert de Burgh got ships together and sunk many vessels, and drove the others back in the Straits of Dover; so that Louis was forced to go home and leave England in peace.

Henry must have been too young to understand about Magna Carta when he swore to it, but it was the trouble of all his long reign to get him to observe it. It was not that he was wicked like his father – for he was very religious and kind-hearted – but he was too good-natured, and never could say No to anybody. Bad advisers got about him when he grew up, and persuaded him to let them take good Hubert de Burgh and imprison him. He had taken refuge in a church, but they dragged him out and took him to a blacksmith to have chains put on his feet; the smith however said he would never forge chains for the man who had saved his country from the French. De Burgh was afterwards set free, and died in peace and honor.

Henry was a builder of beautiful churches. Westminster Abbey, as it is now, was one. And he was so charitable to the poor that, when he had his children weighed, he gave their weight in gold and silver in alms. But he gave to everyone who asked, and so always wanted money; and sometimes his men could get nothing for the king and queen to eat, but by going and taking sheep and poultry from the poor farmers around; so that things were nearly as bad as under William Rufus – because the king was foolishly good-natured. The Pope was always sending for money, too; and the king tried to raise it in ways that, according to Magna Carta, he had sworn not to do. His foreign friends told him that if he minded Magna Carta he would be a poor creature – not like a king who might do all he pleased; and whenever he listened to them he broke the laws of Magna Carta. Then, when his barons complained and frightened him, he swore again to keep them; so that nobody could trust him, and his weakness was almost as bad for the kingdom as John's wickedness. When they could bear it no longer, the barons all met him at the council which was called the Parliament, from a French word meaning talk. This time they came in armor, bringing all their fighting men, and declared that he had broken his word so often that they should appoint some of their own number to watch him, and hinder his doing anything against the laws he had sworn to observe, or from getting money from the people without their consent. He was very angry; but he was in their power, and had to submit to swear that so it should be; and Simon de Montfort, Earl of Leicester, who had married his sister, was appointed among the lords who were to keep watch over him. Henry could not bear this; he felt himself to be less than ever a king, and tried to break loose. He had never cared for his promises; but his brave son Edward, who was now grown up, cared a great deal: and they put the question to Louis, King of France, whether the king was bound by the oath he had made to be under Montfort and his council. This Louis was son to the one who had been driven back by Hubert de Burgh. He was one of the best men and kings that ever lived, and he tried to judge rightly; but he scarcely thought how much provocation Henry had given, when he said that subjects had no right to frighten their king, and so that Henry and Edward were not obliged to keep the oath.

Thereupon they got an army together, and so did Simon de Montfort and the barons; and they met at a place called Lewes, in Sussex. Edward got the advantage at first, and galloped away, driving his enemies before him; but when he turned round and came back, he found that Simon de Montfort had beaten the rest of the army, and made his father and uncle Richard prisoners. Indeed, the barons threatened to cut off Richard's head if Edward went on fighting with them; and to save his uncle's life, he too, gave himself up to them.

Simon de Montfort now governed all the kingdom. He still called Henry king, but did not let him do anything, and watched him closely that he might not get away; and Edward was kept a prisoner – first in one castle, then in another. Simon was a good and high-minded man himself, who only wanted to do what was best for everyone; but he had a family of proud and overbearing sons, who treated all who came in their way so ill, that most of the barons quarreled with them. One of these barons sent Edward a beautiful horse; and one day when he was riding out from Hereford Castle with his keepers, he proposed to them to ride races, while he was to look on and decide which was the swiftest. Thus they all tired out their horses, and as soon as he saw that they could hardly get them along, Edward spurred his own fresh horse, and galloped off to meet the friends who were waiting for him. All who were discontented with the Montforts joined him, and he soon had a large army. He marched against Montfort, and met him at Evesham. The poor old king was in Montfort's army, and in the battle was thrown down, and would have been killed if he had not called out – "Save me, save me, I am Henry of Winchester." His son heard the call, and, rushing to his side, carried him to a place of safety. His army was much the strongest, and Montfort had known from the first that there was no hope for him. "God have mercy on our souls, for our bodies are Sir Edward's," he had said; and he died bravely on the field of battle.

Edward brought his father back to reign in all honor, but he took the whole management of the kingdom, and soon set things in order again – taking care that Magna Carta should be properly observed. When everything was peaceful at home, he set out upon a Crusade with the good King of France, and while he was gone his father died, after a reign of fifty-six years. There only three English Kings who reigned more than fifty years, and these are easy to remember, as each was the third of his name – Henry III., Edward III., and George III. In the reign of Henry III. the custom of having Parliaments was established, and the king was prevented from getting money from the people unless the Parliament granted it. The Parliament has, ever since, been made up of great lords, who are born to it: and, besides them, of men chosen by the people in the counties and towns, to speak and decide for them. The clergy have a meeting of their own called Convocation; and these three – Clergy, Lords, and Commons – are called the Three Estates of the Realm.

CHAPTER XV.

EDWARD I., LONGSHANKS. A.D. 1272 – 1307.

The son of Henry III. returned from the Holy Land to be one of our noblest, best, and wisest kings. Edward I. – called Longshanks in a kind of joke, because he was the tallest man in the Court – was very grand-looking and handsome; and could leap, run, ride, and fight in his heavy armor better than anyone else. He was brave, just, and affectionate; and his sweet wife, Eleanor of Castille, was warmly loved by him and all the nation. He built as many churches and was as charitable as his father, but he was much more careful to make only good men bishops, and he allowed no wasting or idling. He faithfully obeyed Magna Carta, and made everyone else obey the law – indeed many good laws and customs have begun from this time. Order was the great thing he cared for, and under him the English grew prosperous and happy, when nobody was allowed to rob them.

The Welsh were, however, terrible robbers. You remember that they are the remains of the old Britons, who used to have all Britain. They had never left off thinking that they had a right to it, and coming down out of their mountains to burn the houses and steal the cattle of the Saxons, as they still called the English. Edward tried to make friends with their princes – Llewellyn and David – and to make them keep their people in order. He gave David lands in England, and let Llewellyn marry his cousin, Eleanor de Montfort. But they broke their promises shamefully, and did such savage things to the English on their borders that he was forced to put a stop to it, and went to war. David was made prisoner, and put to death as a traitor; and Llewellyn was met by some soldiers near the bridge of Builth and killed, without their knowing who he was. Edward had, in the meantime, conquered most of the country; and he told the Welsh chiefs that, if they would come and meet him at Caernarvon Castle, he would give them a prince who had been born in their country – had never spoken a word of any language but theirs. They all came, and the king came down to them with his own little baby son in his arms, who had lately been born in Caernarvon Castle, and, of course, had never spoken any language at all. The Welsh were obliged to accept him; and he had a Welsh nurse, that the first words he spoke might be Welsh. They thought he would have been altogether theirs, as he then had an elder brother; but in a year or two the oldest boy died; and, ever since that time, the eldest son of the King of England has always been Prince of Wales.

There was a plan for the little Prince Edward of Caernarvon being married to a little girl, who was grand-daughter to the King of Scotland, and would be Queen of Scotland herself – and this would have led to the whole island being under one king – but, unfortunately, the little maiden died. It was so hard to decide who ought to reign, out of all her cousins, that they asked king Edward to choose among them – since everyone knew that a great piece of Scotland belonged to him as over-lord, just as his own dukedom of Aquitaine belonged to the King of France over him; and the Kings of Scotland always used to pay homage to those of England for it.

Edward chose John Balliol, the one who had the best right; but he made him understand that, as overlord, he meant to see that as good order was kept in

Scotland as in England. Now, the English kings had never meddled with Scottish affairs before, and the Scots were furious at finding that he did so. They said it was insulting them and their king; and poor Balliol did not know what to do among them, but let them defy Edward in his name. This brought Edward and his army to Scotland. The strong places were taken and filled with English soldiers, and Balliol was made prisoner, adjudged to have rebelled against his lord and forfeited his kingdom, and was sent away to France.

Edward thought it would be much better for the whole country to join Scotland to England, and rule it himself. And so, no doubt, it would have been; but many Scots were not willing, – and in spite of all the care he could take, the soldiers who guarded his castles often behaved shamefully to the people round them. One gentleman, named William Wallace, whose home had been broken up by some soldiers, fled to the woods and hills, and drew so many Scots round him that he had quite an army. There was a great fight at the Bridge of Stirling; the English governors were beaten, and Wallace led his men over the border into Northumberland, where they plundered and burnt wherever they went, in revenge for what had been done in Scotland.

Edward gathered his forces and came to Scotland. The army that Wallace had drawn together could not stand before him, but was defeated at Falkirk, and Wallace had to take to the woods. Edward promised pardon to all who would submit – and almost all did; but Wallace still lurked in the hills, till one of his own countrymen betrayed him to the English, when he was sent to London, and put to death.

All seemed quieted, and English garrisons – that

is, guarding soldiers – were in all the Scottish towns and castles, when, suddenly, Robert Bruce, one of the half English, half Scottish nobles between whom Edward had judged, ran away from the English court, with his horse's shoes put on backwards. The next thing that was heard of him was, that he had quarreled with one of his cousins in the church at Dumfries, and stabbed him to the heart, and then had gone to Scone and had been crowned King of Scotland.

Edward was bitterly angry now. He sent on an army to deal unsparingly with the rising, and set out to follow with his son, now grown to man's estate. Crueller things than he had ever allowed before were done to the places where Robert Bruce had been acknowledged as king, and his friends were hung as traitors wherever they were found; but Bruce himself could not be caught. He was living a wild life among the lakes and hills; and Edward, who was an old man now, had been taken so ill at Carlisle, that he could not come on to keep his own strict rule among his men. All the winter he lay sick there; and in the spring he heard that Bruce, whom he thought quite crushed, had suddenly burst upon the English, defeated them, and was gathering strength every day.

Edward put on his armor and set out for Scotland; but at Burgh-on- the-Sands his illness came on again, and he died there at seventy years old.

He was buried in Westminster Abbey, under a great block of stone, and the inscription on it only says, "Edward I., 1308 – The Hammer of the Scots – Keep Treaties." His good wife, Queen Eleanor, had died many years before him, and was also buried at Westminster. All the way from Grantham, in Lincolnshire – where she died – to London, Edward set up a beautiful stone cross wherever her body rested for the night – fifteen of them – but only three are left now.

CHAPTER XVI.

EDWARD II., OF CAERNARVON. A.D. 1307 – 1327.

Unlike his father in everything was the young Edward, who had just come to manhood in mind, for he was silly and easily led as his grandfather, Henry III., had been. He had a friend - a gay, handsome, thoughtless, careless young man - named Piers Gaveston, who had often led him into mischief. His father had banished this dangerous companion, and forbidden, under pain of his heaviest displeasure, the two young men from ever meeting again; but the moment the old king was dead, Edward turned back from Scotland, where he was so much wanted, and sent for Piers Gaveston again. At the same time his bride arrived - Isabel, daughter to the King of France, a beautiful girl - and there was a splendid wedding feast; but the king and Gaveston were both so vain and conceited, that they cared more about their own beauty and fine dress than the young queen's, and she found herself quite neglected. The nobles, too, were angered at the airs that Gaveston gave himself; he not only dressed splendidly, had a huge train of servants, and managed the king as he pleased, but he was very insolent to them, and gave them nick-names. He called the king's cousin, the Earl of Lancaster, "the old hog;" the Earl of Pembroke, "Joseph the Jew;" and the Earl of Warwick, "the black dog." Meantime, the king and he were wasting the treasury, and doing harm of all kinds, till the barons gathered together and forced the king to send his favorite into banishment. Gaveston went, but he soon came back again and joined the king, who was at last setting out for Scotland.

The nobles, however, would not endure his return. they seized him, brought him to Warwick Castle, and there held a kind of Court, which could hardly be called of Justice, for they had no right at all to sentence him. He spoke them fair now, and begged hard for his life; but they could not forget the names he had called them, and he was beheaded on Blacklow Hill.

Edward was full of grief and anger for the cruel death of his friend; but he was forced to keep it out of sight, for all the barons were coming round him for the Scottish war. While he had been wasting his time, Robert Bruce had obtained every strong place in Scotland, except Stirling Castle, and there the English governor had promised to yield, if succor did not come from England within a year and a day.

The year was almost over when Edward came into Scotland with a fine army of English, Welsh, and Gascons from Aquitaine; but Robert Bruce was a great and able general, and he was no general at all; so when the armies met at Bannockburn, under the walls of Stirling, the English were worse beaten than ever they had been anywhere else, except at Hastings. Edward was obliged to flee away to England, and though Bruce was never owned by the English to be King of Scotland, there he really reigned, having driven every Englishman away, and taken all the towns and castles. Indeed, the English had grown so much afraid of the Scots, that a hundred would flee at the sight of two.

The king comforted himself with a new friend – Hugh le Despencer – who, with his old father, had his own way, just like Gaveston. Again the barons rose, and required that they should be banished. They went, but the Earl of Lancaster carried his turbulence too far, and, when he hear that the father had come back, raised an army, and was even found to have asked Robert Bruce to help him against his own king. This made the other barons so angry that they joined the king against him, and he was made prisoner and put to death for making war on the king, and making friends with the enemies of the country.

Edward had his Le Despencers back again, and very discontented the sight made the whole country – and especially the queen, whom he had always neglected, though she now had four children. He had never tried to gain her love, and she hated him more and more. There was some danger of a quarrel with her brother, the King of France, and she offered to go with her son Edward, now about fourteen, and settle it. But this was only an excuse. She went about to the princes abroad, telling them how ill she was used by her husband, and asking for help. A good many knights believed and pitied her, and came with her to England to help. All the English who hated the Le Despencers joined her, and she led the young prince against his father. Edward and his friends were hunted across into Wales; but they were tracked out one by one, and the Despencers were put to a cruel death, though Edward gave himself up in hopes of saving them.

The queen and her friends made him own that he did not deserve to reign, and would give up the crown to his son. Then they kept him in prison, taking him from one castle to another, in great misery. The rude soldiers of his guard mocked him and crowned him with hay, and gave him dirty ditch water to shave with; and when they found he was too strong and healthy to die only of bad food and damp lodging, they murdered him one night in Berkeley Castle.

He lies buried in Gloucester Cathedral, not far from that other foolish and unfortunate prince, Robert of Normandy. He had reigned twenty years, and was dethroned in 1327.

The queen then wanted to get rid of Edmund, Earl of Kent, the poor king's youngest brother. So a report was spread that Edward was alive, and Edmund was allowed to peep into a dark prison room, where he saw a man who he thought was his brother. He tried to stir up friends to set the king free; but this was called rebelling, and he was taken and beheaded at Winchester by a criminal condemned to die, for it was such a wicked sentence that nobody else could be found to carry it out.

CHAPTER XVII.

EDWARD III. A.D. 1327 – 1377.

For about three years, the cruel Queen Isabel and her friends managed all the country; but as soon as her son – Edward III., who had been crowned instead of his father – understood how wicked she had been, and was strong enough to deal with her party, he made them prisoners, put the worst of them to death, and kept the queen shut up in a castle as long as she lived. He had a very good queen of his own, named Phillipa, who brought cloth-workers over from he own country Hainault (now part of Belgium), to teach the English their trade, and thus began to render England the chief country in the world for wool and cloth.

Queen Isabel, Edward's mother, had, you remember, been daughter of the King of France. All her three brothers died without leaving a son, and their cousin, whose name was Philip, began to reign in their stead. Edward, however, fancied that the crown of France properly belonged to him, in right of his mother; but he did not stir about it at once, and, perhaps, never would have done so at all, but for two things. One was, that the King of France, Philip VI., had been so foolish as to fancy that one of his lords, named Robert of Artois, had been bewitching him – by sticking pins into a wax figure and roasting it before the fire. So this Robert was driven out of France and, coming to England, stirred Edward up to go and overthrow Philip. The other was, that the English barons had grown so restless and troublesome, that they would not stay peacefully at home and mind their own estate; – but if they had not wars abroad, they always gave the king trouble at home; and Edward liked better that they should fight for him than against him. So he called himself King of France and England, and began a war which lasted – with short space of quiet – for full one hundred years, and only ended in the time of the great grandchildren of the men who entered upon it. There was one great sea-fight off Sluys, when the king sat in his ship, in a black velvet dress, and gained a great victory; but it was a good while before there was any great battle by land – so long, that the king's eldest son, Edward Prince of Wales, was sixteen years old. He is generally called the Black Prince – no one quite knows why, for his hair, like that of all these old English kings, was quite light and his eyes were blue. He was such a spirited young soldier, that when the French army under King Philip came in sight of the English one, near the village of Crecy, King Edward said he should have the honor of the day, and stood under a windmill on a his watching the fight, while the prince led the English army. He gained a very great victory, and in the evening came and knelt before his father, saying the praise was not his own but the king's, who had ordered all so wisely. Afterwards, while Philip had fled away, Edward besieged Calais, the town just opposite to Dover. The inhabitants were very brave, and held out for a long time; and while Edward was absent, the Scots under David, the son of Robert Bruce, came over the Border, and began to burn and plunder in Northumberland. However, Phillipa could be brave in time of need. She did not send for her husband, but called an army together, and the Scots were so well beaten at Neville's Cross, that their king, David himself, was obliged to give himself up to an English squire. The man would not let the queen have his prisoner, but rode day and night to Dover, and then crossed to Calais to tell the king, who bade him put King David into Queen

Philippa's keeping. She came herself to the camp, just as the brave men of Calais had been starved out; and Edward had said he would only consent not to burn the town down, if six of the chief townsmen would bring him the keys of the gates, kneeling, with sackcloth on, and halters round their necks, ready to be hung. Queen Philippa wept when she saw them, and begged that they might be spared; and when the king granted them to her she had them led away, and gave each a good dinner and a fresh suit of clothes. The king, however, turned all the French people out of Calais, and filled it with English, and it remained quite an English town for more than 200 years.

King Philip VI. of France died, and his son John became king, while still the war went on. The Black Prince and John had a terrible battle at a place called Poitiers, and the English gained another victory. King John and one of his sons were made prisoners, but when they were brought to the tent where the Black Prince was to sup, he made them sit down at the table before him, and waited on them as if they had been his guests instead of his prisoners. He did all he could to prevent captivity being a pain to them; and when he brought them to London, he gave John a tall white horse to ride, and only rode a small pony himself by his side. There were two kings prisoners in the Tower of London, and they were treated as if they were visitors and friends. John was allowed to go home, provided he would pay a ransom by degrees, as he could get the money together; and, in the meantime, his two elder sons were to be kept at Calais in his stead. But they would not stay at Calais, and King John could not obtain the sum for his ransom; so, rather than cheat King Edward, he went back to his prison in England again. He died soon after; and his son

Charles was a cleverer and wiser man, who knew it was better not to fight battles with the English, but made a truce, or short peace.

Prince Edward governed that part of the south of France that belonged to his father; but he went on a foolish expedition into Spain, to help a very bad king whom his subjects had driven out, and there caught an illness from which he never quite recovered. While he was ill King Charles began the war again; and, though there was no battle, he tormented the English, and took the castles and towns they held. The Black Prince tried to fight, but he was too weak and ill to do much, and was obliged to go home, and leave the government to his brother John, Duke of Lancaster. He lived about six years after he came home, and then died, to the great sorrow of everyone. His father, King Edward, was now too old and feeble to attend to the affairs of the country. Queen Philippa was dead too, and as no one took proper care of the poor old king, he fell into the hands of bad servants, who made themselves rich and neglected him. When, at length, he lay dying, they stole the ring off his finger before he had breathed his last, and left him all alone, with the doors open, till a priest came by, and stayed and prayed by him till his last moment. He had reigned exactly fifty years. You had better learn and remember the names of his sons, as you will hear more about some of them. They were Edward, Lionel, John, Edmund, and Thomas. Edward was Prince of Wales; Lionel, Duke of Clarence; John, Duke of Lancaster; Edmund, Duke of York; and Thomas, Duke of Gloucester. Edward and Lionel both died before their father. Edward had left a son named Richard; Lionel had left a daughter named Philippa.

CHAPTER XVIII.

RICHARD II. A.D. 1377 – 1399.

These were not very good times in England. The new King, Richard, was only eleven years old, and his three uncles did not care much for his good or the good of the nation. There was not much fighting going on in France, but for the little there was a great deal of money was wanting, and the great lords were apt to be very hard upon the poor people on their estates. They would not let them be taught to read; and if a poor man who belonged to an estate went away to a town, his lord could have him brought back to his old home. Any tax, too, fell more heavily on the poor than the rich. One tax, especially, called the poll tax, which was made when Richard was sixteen, vexed them greatly. Everyone above fifteen years old had to pay fourpence, and the collectors were often very rude and insolent. A man named Wat Tyler, in Kent, was so angry with a rude collector as to strike him dead. All the villagers came together with sticks, scythes, and flails; and Wat Tyler told them they would go to London, and tell the king how his poor commons were treated. More people and more joined them on the way, and an immense multitude of wild looking men came pouring into London, where the Lord Mayor and Aldermen were taken by surprise, and could do nothing to stop them. They did not do much harm then; they lay on the grass all night round the Tower, and said they wanted to speak to the king. In the morning he came down to his barge, and meant to have spoken to them; but his people, seeing such a host of wild men, took fright, and carried him back again. He went out again the next day on horseback; but while he was speaking to some of them, the worst of them broke into the Tower, where they seized

Archbishop Simon of Canterbury, and fancying he was one of the king's bad advisers, they cut off his head. Richard had to sleep in the house called the Royal Wardrobe that night, but he went out again on horseback among the mob, and began trying to understand what they wanted. Wat Tyler, while talking, grew violent, forgot to whom he was speaking, and laid his hand on the king's bridle, as if to threaten or take him prisoner. Upon this, the Lord Mayor, with his mace – the large crowned staff that is carried before him – dealt the man such a blow that fell from his horse, and an attendant thrust him through with a sword. The people wavered, and seemed not to know what to do: and the young king, with great readiness, rode forward and said – "Good fellows, have you lost your leader? This fellow was but a traitor, I am your king, and will be your captain and guide." Then he rode at their head out into the fields, and the gentlemen, who had mustered their men by this time, were able to get between them and the city. The people of each county were desired to state their grievances; the king engaged to do what he could for them, and they went home.

Richard seems to have really wished to take away some of the laws that were so hard upon them, but his lords would not let him, and he had as yet very little power – being only a boy – and by the time he grew up his head was full of vanity and folly. He was very handsome, and he cared more for fine clothes and amusements than for business; and his youngest uncle, the Duke of Gloucester, did all he could to keep him back, and hinder him from taking his affairs into his own hands. Not till he was twenty-four did Richard begin to govern for himself; and then the Duke of Gloucester was always grumbling and setting the people to grumble, because the king chose to have peace with France.

Duke Thomas used to lament over the glories of the battles of Edward III., and tell the people they had taxes to pay to keep the king in ermine robes, and rings, and jewels, and to let him give feasts and tilting matches – when the knights, in beautiful, gorgeous armor, rode against one another in sham fight, and the king and ladies looked on and gave the prize.

Now, Richard knew very well that all this did not cost half so much as his grandfather's wars, and he said it did not signify to the people what he wore, or how he amused himself, as long as he did not tax them and take their lambs and sheaves to pay for it. But the people would not believe him, and Gloucester was always stirring them up against him, and interfering with him in council. At last, Richard went as if on a visit to his uncle at Pleshy Castle; and there, in his own presence, caused him to be seized and sent off to Calais. In a few days' time Thomas, Duke of Gloucester, was dead; and to this day nobody knows whether his grief and rage brought on a fit, or if he was put to death. It is certain, at least, that Richard's other two uncles do not seem to have treated the king as if he had been to blame. The elder of these uncles, the Duke of Lancaster, was called John of Gaunt – because he had been born a Ghent, a town in Flanders. He was becoming an old man, and only tried to help the king and keep things quiet; but Henry, his eldest son, was a fine high-spirited young man – a favorite with everybody, and was always putting himself forward – and the king was very much afraid of him.

One day, when Parliament met, the king stood up, and commanded Henry of Lancaster to tell all those present what the Duke of Norfolk had said when they were riding together. Henry gave in a written paper, saying that the duke had told him that they should all be ruined, like the Duke of Gloucester, and that the king would find some way to destroy them. Norfolk angrily sprang up, and declared he had said no such thing. In those days, when no one could tell which spoke the truth, the two parties often would offer to fight, and it was believed that God would show the right, by giving the victory to the sincere one. So Henry and Norfolk were to fight; but just as they were mounted on their horses, with their lances in their hands, the king threw down his staff before them, stopped the combat, and sentenced Norfolk to be banished from England for life, and Henry for ten years.

Not long after Henry had gone, his old father – John of Gaunt – died, and the king kept all his great dukedom of Lancaster. Henry would not bear this, and knew that many people at home thought it very unfair; so he came to England, and as soon as he landed at Ravenspur in Yorkshire, people flocked to him so eagerly, that he began to think he could do more than make himself duke of Lancaster. King Richard was in Ireland, where his cousin, the governor – Roger Mortimer – had been killed by the wild Irish. He came home in haste on hearing of Henry's arrival, but everybody turned against him: and the Earl of Northumberland, whom he had chiefly trusted, made him prisoner and carried him to Henry. He was taken to London, and there set before Parliament, to confess that he had ruled so ill that he was unworthy to reign, and gave up the crown to his dear cousin Henry of Lancaster, in the year 1399.

Then he was sent away to Pontefract Castle, and what happened to him there nobody knows, but he never came out of it alive.

CHAPTER XIX.

HENRY IV. A.D. 1399 – 1413.

The English people had often chosen their king out of the royal family in old times, but from John to Richard II., he had always been the son and heir of the last king. Now, though poor Richard had no child, Henry of Lancaster was not the next of kin to him, for Lionel, Duke of Clarence, had come between the Black Prince and John of Gaunt; and his great grandson, Edmund Mortimer, was thought by many to have a better right to be king than Henry. Besides, people did not know whether Richard was alive, and they thought him hardly used, and wanted to set him free. So Henry had a very uneasy time. Everyone had been fond of him when he was a bright, friendly, free-spoken noble, and he thought that he would be a good king and much loved; but he had gained the crown in an evil way, and it never gave him any peace or joy. The Welsh, who always had loved Richard, took up arms for him, and the Earl of Northumberland, who had betrayed Richard, expected a great deal too much from Henry. The earl had a brave son – Henry Percy – who was so fiery and eager that he was commonly called Hotspur. He was sent to fight with the Welsh: and with the king's son, Henry, Prince of Wales – a brave boy of fifteen or sixteen – under his charge, to teach him the art of war; and they used to climb the mountains and sleep in tents together as good friends.

But the Scots made an attack on England. Henry Percy went north to fight with them, and beat them in a great battle, making many prisoners. The King sent to ask to have the prisoners sent to London, and this made the proud Percy so angry that he gave up the cause of King Henry, and went off to Wales, taking his prisoners with him; and there – being by this time nearly sure that poor Richard must be dead – he joined the Welsh in choosing, as the only right king of England, young Edmund Mortimer. Henry IV. and his sons gathered an army easily – for the Welsh were so savage and cruel, that the English were sure to fight against them if they broke into England. The battle was fought near Shrewsbury. It was a very fierce one, and in it Hotspur was killed, the Welsh put to flight, and the Prince of Wales fought so well that everyone saw he was likely to be a brave, warlike king, like Edward I. or Edward III.

The troubles were not over, however, for the Earl of Northumberland himself, and Archbishop Scrope of York, took up arms against the king; but they were put down without a battle. The Earl fled and hid himself, but the archbishop was taken and beheaded – the first bishop whom a king of England had ever put to death. The Welsh went on plundering and doing harm, and Prince Henry had to be constantly on the watch against them; and, in fact, there never was a reign so full of plots and conspiracies. The king never knew whom to trust: one friend after another turned against him, and he became soured and wretched: he was worn out with disappointment and guarding against everyone, and at last he grew even suspicious of his brave son Henry, because he was so bright and bold, and was so much loved. The prince was ordered home from Wales, and obliged to live at Windsor, with nothing to do, while his youngest brothers were put before him and trusted by their father – one of them even sent to command the army in France. But happily the four brothers – Henry, Thomas, John and

Humfrey – all loved each other so well that nothing could make them jealous or at enmity with one another. At Windsor, too, the king kept young Edmund Mortimer – whom the Welsh had tried to make king, – and also the young English princes, and they all led a happy life together.

There are stories told of Henry – Prince Hal, as he was called – leading a wild, merry life, as a sort of madcap; playing at being a robber, and breaking into the wagons that were bringing treasure for his father, and then giving the money back again. Also there is a story that, when one of his friends was taken before the Lord Chief Justice, he went and ordered him to be released and that when the justice refused he drew his sword, upon which the justice sent him to prison; and he went quietly, knowing it was right. The king is said to have declared himself happy to have a judge who maintained the law so well, and a son who would submit to it; but there does not seem to be good reason for believing the story; and it seems clear that young Henry, if he was full of fun and frolic, took care never to do anything really wrong.

The king was an old man before his time. He was always ill, and often had fits, and one of these came on when he was in Westminster Abbey. He was taken to the room called the Jerusalem chamber, and Henry watched him there. Another of the stories is that the king lay as if he were dead, and the prince took the crown that was by his side and carried it away. When the king revived, Henry brought it back, with many excuses. "Ah, fair son," said the king, "what right have you to the crown? you know your father had none."

"Sir," said Henry, "with your sword you took it, and with my sword I will keep it."

"May God have mercy on my soul," said the king.

Another story tells show the prince, feeling that his father doubted his loyalty, presented himself one day in disordered attire before the king, and kneeling, offered him a dagger, and begged his father to take his life, if he could no longer trust and love him.

We cannot be quite certain about the truth of these conversations, for many people will write down stories they have heard, without making sure of them. One thing we are certain of which Henry told his son, which seems less like repentance. It was that, unless he made war in France, his lords would never let him be quiet on his throne in England; and this young Henry was quite ready to believe. There had never been a real peace between France and England since Edward III. had begun the war – only truces, which are short rests in the middle of a great war – and the English were eager to begin again; for people seldom thought then of the misery that comes of a great war, but only of the honor and glory that were to be gained, of making prisoners and getting ransoms from them.

So Henry IV. died, after having made his own life miserable by taking the crown unjustly, and, as you will see, leaving a great deal or harm still to come to the whole country, as well as to France.

He died in the year 1399. His family is called the House of Lancaster, because his father had been Duke of Lancaster. You will be amused to hear that Richard Whittington really lived in his time. I cannot answer for his cat, but he was really Lord Mayor of London, and supplied the wardrobe of King Henry's daughter, when she married the King of Denmark.

CHAPTER XX.

HENRY V., OF MONMOUTH. A.D. 1413 – 1423.

The young King Henry was full of high, good thoughts. He was devout in going to church, tried to make good Bishops, gave freely to the poor, and was so kindly, and hearty, and merry in all his words and ways, that everyone loved him. Still, he thought it was his duty to go and make war in France. He had been taught to believe the kingdom belonged to him, and it was in so wretched a state that he thought he could do it good. The poor king, Charles VI., was mad, and had a wicked wife besides; and his sons, and uncles, and cousins were always fighting, till the streets of Paris were often red with blood, and the whole country was miserable. Henry hoped to set all in order for them, and gathering an army together, crossed to Normandy. He called on the people to own him as their true king, and never let any harm be done to them, for he hung any soldier who was caught stealing, or misusing anyone. He took the town of Harfleur, on the coast of Normandy, but not till after a long siege, when his camp was in so wet a place that there was much illness among his men. The store of food was nearly used up, and he was obliged to march his troops across to Calais, which you know belonged to England, to get some more. But on the way the French army came up to meet him – a very grand, splendid-looking army, commanded by the king's eldest son the dauphin. Just as the English kings' eldest son was always Prince of Wales, the French kings' eldest son was always called Dauphin of Vienne, because Vienne, the country that belonged to him, had a dolphin on its shield. The French army was very large – quite twice the number of the English – but, though Henry's men were weary and half-starved, and many of them sick, they were not afraid, but believed their king when he told them that there were enough Frenchmen to kill, enough to run away, enough to make prisoners. At night, however, the English had solemn prayers, and made themselves ready, and the king walked from tent to tent to see that each man was in his place; while, on the other hand, the French were feasting and revelling, and settling what they would do the English when they had made them prisoners. They were close to a little village which the English called Agincourt, and, though that is not quite its right name, it is what we have called the battle ever since. The French, owing to the quarrelsome state of the country, had no order or obedience among them. Nobody would obey any other; and when their own archers were in the way, the horsemen began cutting them down as if they were the enemy. Some fought bravely, but it was of little use; and by night all the French were routed, and King Henry's banner waving in victory over the field. He went back to England in great glory, and all the aldermen of London came out to meet him in red gowns and gold chains, and among them was Sir Richard Whittington, the great silk mercer.

Henry was so modest that he would not allow the helmet he had worn at Agincourt, all knocked about with terrible blows, to be carried before him when he rode into London, and he went straight to church, to give thanks to God for his victory. He soon went back to France, and went on conquering it till the queen came to an agreement with him that he should marry his daughter Catherine, and that, though poor, crazy Charles VI. should reign to the end of his life, when he died Henry and Catherine should be king and queen of France. So Henry and Catherine were married, and he took her home to England with great joy and pomp, leaving his brother Thomas, Duke of Clarence to take care of his army in France. For, of course, though the queen had made this treaty for her mad husband, most brave, honest Frenchmen could not but feel it a wicked and unfair thing to give the kingdom away from her son, the Dauphin Charles. He was not a good man, and had consented to the murder of his cousin, the Duke of Burgundy, and this had turned some against him; but still he was badly treated, and the bravest Frenchmen could not bear to see their country given up to the English. So, though he took no trouble to fight for himself, they fought for him, and got some Scots to help them; and by and by news came to Henry that his army had been beaten, and his brother killed.

He came back again in haste to France, and his presence made everything go well again; but all the winter he was besieging the town of Meaux, where there was a very cruel robber, who made all the roads to Paris unsafe, and by the time he had taken it his health was much injured. His queen came to him, and they kept a very grand court at Paris, at Whitsuntide; but soon after, when Henry set out to join his army, he found himself so ill and weak that he was obliged to turn back to the Castle of Vincennes, where he grew much worse. He called for all his friends, and begged them to be faithful to his little baby son, whom he had never even seen; and he spoke especially to his brother John, Duke of Bedford, to whom he left the charge of all he had gained. He had tried to be a good man, and though his attack on France was really wrong, and caused great misery, he had meant to do right. So he was not afraid to face death, and he died when only thirty-four years old, while he was listening to the 51st Psalm. Everybody grieved for him – even the French – and nobody had ever been so good and dutiful to poor old King Charles, who sat in a corner lamenting for his good son Henry, and wasting away till he died, only three weeks later, so that he was buried the same day, at St. Denys Abbey, near Paris, as Henry was buried at Westminster Abbey, near London.

CHAPTER XXI.

HENRY VI., OF WINDSOR. A.D. 1423 – 1461.

The poor little baby, Henry VI., was but nine months old when – over the grave of his father in England, and his grandfather in France – he was proclaimed King of France and England. The crown of England was held over his head, and his lords made their oaths to him: and when he was nine years old he was sent to Paris, and there crowned King of France. He was a very good, little, gentle boy, as meek and obedient as possible; but his friends, who knew that a king must be brave, strong, and firm for his people's sake, began to be afraid that nothing would ever make him manly. The war in France went on all the time: the Duke of Bedford keeping the north and the old lands in the south-west for little Henry, and the French doing their best for their rightful king – though he was so lazy and fond of pleasure that he let them do it all alone.

Yet a wonderful thing happened in his favor. The English were besieging Orleans, when a young village girl, named Joan of Arc, came to King Charles and told him that she had had a commission from Heaven to save Orleans, and to lead him to Rheims, where French kings were always crowned. And she did! She always acted as one led by Heaven. Many wonderful things are told of her, and one circumstance that produced a great impression on the public mind was that when brought into the presence of Charles, whom she had never before seen, she recognized him, although he was dressed plainly, and one of the courtiers had on the royal apparel. She never let anything wrong be done in her sight – no bad words spoken, no savage deeds done; and she never fought herself, only led the French soldiers. The English thought her a witch, and fled like sheep whenever they saw her; and the French common men were always brave with her to lead them. And so she really saved Orleans, and brought the king to be crowned at Rheims. But neither Charles nor his selfish bad nobles liked her. She was too good for them; so, though they would not let her go home to her village as she wished, they gave her no proper help; and once, when there was a fight going on outside the walls of a town, the French all ran away and left her outside, where she was taken by the English. And then, I grieve to say, the court that sat to judge her – some English and some French of the English party – sentenced her to be burnt to death in the market place at Rouen as a witch, and her own king never tried to save her.

But the spirit she had stirred up never died away. The French went on winning back more and more; and there were so many quarrels among the English that they had little chance of keeping anything. The king's youngest uncle, Humfrey, Duke of Gloucester, was always disputing with the Beaufort family. John of Gaunt, Duke of Lancaster – father to Henry IV. – had, late in life, married a person of low birth, and her children were called Beaufort, after the castle where they were born – not Plantagenet – and were hardly reckoned as princes by other people; but they were very proud, and thought themselves equal to anybody. The good Duke of Bedford died quite worn out with trying to keep the peace among them, and to get proper help from England to save the lands his brother had won in France. All this time, the king liked the Beauforts much better than Duke Humfrey, and he followed their advice, and that of their friend, the Earl the Earl of Suffolk, in marrying Margaret of Anjou – the daughter of a French prince, who had a right to a great part of the lands the English held. All these were given back to her father, and this made the Duke of Gloucester and all the English more angry, and they hated the young queen as the cause. She was as bold and high-spirited as the king was gentle and meek. He loved nothing so well as praying, praising God, and reading; and he did one great thing for the country – which did more for it than all the fighting kings had done – he founded Eton College, close to Windsor Castle; and there many of our best clergymen, and soldiers, and statesmen, have had their education. But while he was happy over rules for his scholars, and in plans for the beautiful chapel, the queen was eagerly taking part in the quarrels, and the nation hated her the more for interfering. And very strangely, Humfrey, Duke of Gloucester, was, at the meeting of Parliament, accused of high treason and sent to prison, where, in a few days, he was found dead in his bed – just like his great-uncle, Thomas, Duke of Gloucester; nor does anyone understand the mystery in one case, better than in the other, except that we are more sure that gentle Henry VI. had nothing to do with it than we can be of Richard II.

These were very bad times. There was a rising like Wat Tyler's, under a man named Jack Cade, who held London for two or three days before he was put down; and, almost at the same time, the queen's first English friend, Suffolk, was exiled by her enemies, and taken at sea and murdered by some sailors. Moreover, the last of the brave old friends of Henry V. was killed in France, while trying to save the remains of the old duchy of Aquitaine, which had belonged to the English kings ever since Henry II. married Queen

Eleanor. That was the end of the hundred years' war, for peace was made at last, and England kept nothing in France but the one city of Calais.

Still things were growing worse. Duke Humfrey left no children, and as time went on and the king had none, the question was who should reign. If the Beauforts were to be counted as princes, they came next; but everyone hated them, so that people recollected that Henry IV. had thrust aside the young Edmund Mortimer, grandson to Lionel, who had been next eldest to the Black Prince. Edmund was dead, but his sister Anne had married a son of the Duke of York, youngest son of Edward III.; and her son Richard, Duke of York, could not help feeling that he had a much better right to be king than any Beaufort. There was a great English noble named Richard Nevil, Earl of Warwick, who liked to manage everything – just the sort of baron that was always mischievous at home, if not fighting in France – and he took up York's cause hotly. York's friends used to wear white roses, Beaufort's friends red roses, and the two parties kept on getting more bitter; but as no one wished any ill to gentle King Henry – who, to make matters worse, sometimes had fits of madness, like his poor grandfather in France – they would hardly have fought it in his lifetime, if he had not at last had a little son, who was born while he was so mad that he did not know of it. Then, when York found it was of no use to wait, he began to make war, backed up by Warwick, and, after much fighting, they made the king prisoner, and forced him to make an agreement that he should reign as long as he lived, but that after that Richard of York should be king, and his son Edward be only Duke of Lancaster. This made the queen furiously angry. She would not give up her son's rights, and she gathered a great army, with which she came suddenly on the Duke of York near Wakefield, and destroyed nearly his whole army. He was killed in the battle; and his second son, Edmund, was met on Wakefield bridge and stabbed by Lord Clifford; and Margaret had their heads set up over the gates of York, while she went on to London to free her husband.

But Edward, York's eldest son, was a better captain than he, and far fiercer and more cruel. He made the war much more savage than it had been before; and after beating the queen's friends at Mortimer's Cross, he hurried on to London, where the people – who had always been very fond of his father, and hated Queen Margaret – greeted him gladly. He was handsome and stately looking; and though he was really cruel when offended, had easy, good-natured manners, and everyone in London was delighted to receive him and own him as king. But Henry and Margaret were in the north with many friends, and he followed them thither to Towton Moor, where, in a snow storm, began the most cruel and savage battle of all the war. Edward gained the victory, and nobody was spared, or made prisoner – all were killed who could not flee. Poor Henry was hidden among his friends, and Margaret went to seek help in Scotland and abroad, taking her son with her. Once she brought another army and fought at Hexham, but she was beaten again; and before long King Henry was discovered by his enemies, carried to London, and shut up a prisoner in the Tower. His reign is reckoned to have ended in 1461.

CHAPTER XXII.

EDWARD IV. A.D. 1461 – 1483.

Though Edward IV. was made king, the wars of the Red and White Roses were not over yet. Queen Margaret and her friends were always trying to get help for poor King Henry. Edward had been so base and mean as to have him led into London, with his feet tied together under his horse, while men struck him on the face, and cried out, "Behold the traitor!" But Henry was meek, patient, and gentle throughout; and, when shut up in the Tower, spent his time in reading and praying, or playing with his little dog.

Queen Margaret and her son Edward were living with her father in France, and she was always trying to have her husband set free, and brought back to his throne. In the meantime, all England was exceeedingly surprised to find that Edward IV. had been secretly married to a beautiful lady named Elizabeth Woodville – Lady Grey. Her first husband had been killed fighting for Henry, and she had stood under an oak tree, when King Edward was passing, to entreat that his lands might not be taken from her little boys. The king fell in love with her and married her, but for a long time he was afraid to tell the Earl of Warwick; and when he did, Warwick was greatly offended – and all the more because Elizabeth's relations were proud and gay in their dress, and tried to set themselves above all the old nobles. Warwick himself had no son, but he had two daughters, whom he meant to marry to the king's two brothers – George, Duke of Clarence, and Richard, Duke of Gloucester. Edward thought this would make Warwick too powerful, and though he could not prevent George from marrying

Isabel Nevil, the eldest daughter, the discontent grew so strong that Warwick persuaded George to fly with him, turn against his own brother, and offer Queen Margaret their help! No wonder Margaret did not trust them, and was very hard to persuade that Warwick could mean well by her; but at last she consented, and gave her son Edward – a fine lad of sixteen – to marry his daughter, Anne Nevil; after which, Warwick – whom men began to call the king-maker – went back to England with Clarence, to raise their men, while she was to follow with her son and his young wife. Warwick came so suddenly that he took the Yorkists at unawares. Edward had to flee for his life to Flanders, leaving his wife and his babies to take shelter in Westminster Abbey – since no one durst take any one out of that holy place – and poor Henry was taken out of prison and set on the throne again. However, Edward soon got help in Flanders, where his sister was married to the Duke of Burgundy. He came back again, gathered his friends, and sent messages to his brother Clarence that he would forgive him if he would desert the earl. No one ever had less faith or honor than George of Clarence. He did desert Warwick, just as the battle of Barnet Heath was beginning; and Warwick's king-making all ended, for he was killed, with his brother and many others, in the battle.

And this was the first news that met Margaret when, after being long hindered by foul weather, she landed at Plymouth. She would have done more wisely to have gone back, but her son Edward longed to strike a blow for his inheritance, and they had friends in Wales whom they hope to meet. So they made their way into Gloucestershire; but there King Edward, with both his brothers, came down upon them at them at Tewkesbury, and there their army was routed, and the young prince taken and killed – some say by the king himself and his brothers. Poor broken hearted Queen Margaret was made prisoner too, and carried to the Tower, where she arrived a day or two after the meek and crazed captive, Henry VI., had been slain, that there might be no more risings in his name. And so ended the long war of York and Lancaster – though not in peace or joy to the savage, faithless family who had conquered.

Edward was merry and good-natured when not angered, and had quite sense and ability enough to have been a very good king, if he had not been lazy, selfish, and full of vices. He actually set out to conquer France, and then let himself be persuaded over and paid off by the cunning King of France, and went home again, a laughing-stock to everybody. The two kings had an interview on a bridge over the River Somme in France, where they talked through a kind of fence, each being too suspicious of the other to meet, without such a barrier between them. As to George, the king had never trusted him since his shameful behavior when Warwick rebelled; besides, he was always abusing the queen's relations, and Richard was always telling the king of all the bad and foolish things he did or said. At last there was a great outbreak of anger, and the king ordered the Duke of Clarence to be imprisoned in the Tower; and there, before long, he too was killed. The saying was that he was drowned in a butt of Malmsey wine, but this is not at all likely to be true. He left two little children, a boy and a girl.

So much cruel slaughter had taken place, that most of the noble families in England had lost many sons, and a great deal of their wealth, and none of them ever became again so mighty as the king-maker had been. His daughter, Anne, the wife of poor Edward of Lancaster, was found by Richard, Duke of Gloucester, hidden as a cook-maid in London, and she was persuaded to marry him – as, indeed, she had always been intended for him. He was a little, thin, slight man, with one shoulder higher than the other, and keen, cunning dark eyes; and as the king was very tall, with a handsome, blue-eyed face, people laughed at the contrast, called Gloucester Richard Crook-back and were very much afraid of him.

It was in this reign that books began to be printed in England instead of written. Printing had been found out in Germany a little before, and books had been shown to Henry VI., but the troubles of his time kept him from attending to them. Now, however, Edward's sister, the Duchess of Burgundy, much encouraged a printer named Caxton, whose books she sent her brother, and other presses were set up in London. Another great change had come in. Long ago, in the time of Henry III., a monk name Roger Bacon had made gunpowder; but nobody used it much until, in the reign of Edward III., it was found out how cannon might be fired with it; and some say it was first used in the battle of Crecy. But it was not till the reign of Edward IV. that smaller guns, such as each soldier could carry one of for himself, were invented – harquebuses, as they were called; – and after this the whole way of fighting was gradually altered. Printing and gunpowder both made great changes in everything, though not all at once. King Edward did not live to see the changes. He had hurt his health with his revellings and amusements, and died quite in middle age, in the year 1483: seeing, perhaps, at last, how much better a king he might have been.

CHAPTER XXIII.

EDWARD V. A.D. 1483.

Edward IV. left several daughters and two sons – Edward, Prince of Wales, who was fourteen years old, and Richard, Duke of York, who was eleven. Edward was at Ludlow Castle – where the princes of Wales were always brought up – with his mother's brother, Lord Rivers; his half- brother, Richard Grey; and other gentlemen.

When the tidings came of his father's death, they set out to bring him to London to be crowned king.

But, in the meantime, the Duke of Gloucester and several of the noblemen, especially the Duke of Buckingham, agreed that it was unbearable that the queen and her brothers should go on having all the power, as they had done in Edward's time. Till the king was old enough to govern, his father's brother, the Duke of Gloucester, was the proper person to rule for him, and they would soon put an end to the Woodvilles. The long wars had made everybody cruel and regardless of the laws, so that no one made much objection when Gloucester and Buckingham met the king and took him from his uncle and half-brother, who were sent off to Pontefract Castle, and in a short time their heads were cut off there. Another of the late king's friends was Lord Hastings; and as he sat at the council table in the Tower of London, with the other lords, Richard came in, and showing his own lean, shrunken arm, declared that Lord Hastings had bewitched him, and made it so. The other lords began to say the *if* he done so it was horrible. But Richard would listen to no *ifs*, and said he would not dine till Hasting's head was off. And his cruel word was done.

The queen saw that harm was intended, and went with all her other children to her former refuge in the sanctuary at Westminster; nor would she leave it when her son Edward rode in state into London and was taken to the Tower, which was then a palace as well as a prison.

The Duke of Gloucester and the Council said that this pretence at fear was very foolish, and that the little Duke of York ought to be with his brother; and they sent the Archbishop of Canterbury to desire her to give the boy up. He found the queen sitting desolate, with all her long light hair streaming about her, and her children round her; and he spoke kindly to her at first and tried to persuade her of what he really believed himself – that it was all her foolish fears and fancies that the Duke of Gloucester could mean any ill to his little nephew, and that the two brothers ought to be together in his keeping.

Elizabeth cried, and said that the boys were better apart, for they quarrelled when they were together, and that she could not give up little Richard. In truth, she guessed that their uncle wanted to get rid of them and to reign himself; and she knew that while she had Richard, Edward would be safe, since it would not make him king to destroy one without the other. Archbishop Morton, who believed Richard's smooth words, and was a very good, kind man, thought this all a woman's nonsense, and told her that if she would not give up the boy freely, he would be taken from her by force. If she had been really a wise, brave mother, she would have gone to the Tower with her boy, as queen and mother, and watched over her children herself. But she had always been a silly, selfish woman, and she was afraid for herself. So she let the archbishop lead her child away, and only sat crying in the sanctuary instead of keeping sight of him.

The next thing that happened was, that the Duke of Gloucester caused one Dr. Shaw to preach a sermon to the people of London in the open air, explaining that King Edward IV. had been a very bad man, and had never been properly married to Lady Grey, and so that she was no queen at all, and her children had no right to reign. The Londoners liked Gloucester and hated the Woodvilles, and all belonging to them, and after some sermons and speeches of this sort, there were so many people inclined to take as their king the man rather than the boy, that the Duke of Buckingham led a deputation to request Richard to accept the crown in his nephew's stead. He met it as if the whole notion was quite new to him, but, of course, accepted the crown, sent for his wife, Anne Nevil, and her son, and was soon crowned as King Richard III. of England.

As for the two boys, they were never seen out of the Tower again. They were sent into the prison part of it, and nobody exactly knows what became of them there; but there cannot be much doubt that they must have been murdered. Some years later, two men confessed that they had been employed to smother the two brothers with pillows, as they slept; and though they added some particulars to the story that can hardly be believed, it is most likely that this was true. Full two hundred years later, a chest was found under a staircase, in what is called the White Tower, containing bones that evidently had belonged to boys of about fourteen and eleven years old; and these were placed in a marble urn among the tombs of the kings in Westminster Abbey. But even to this day, there are some people who doubt whether Edward V. and Richard of York were really murdered, or if Richard were not a person who came back to England and tried to make himself king.

CHAPTER XXIV.

RICHARD III. A.D. 1483 – 1485.

Richard III. seems to have wished to be a good and great king; but he had made his way to the throne in too evil a manner to be likely to prosper. How many people he had put to death we do not know, for when the English began to suspect the he had murdered his two nephews, they also accused him of the death of everyone who had been secretly slain ever since Edward IV. came to the throne, when he had been a mere boy. He found he must be always on the watch; and his home was unhappy, for his son, for whose sake he had striven so hard to be king, died while yet a boy, and Anne, his wife, not long after.

Then his former staunch friend, the Duke of Buckingham, began to feel that though he wanted the sons of Elizabeth Woodville to be set aside from reigning, it was quite another thing to murder them. He was a vain, proud man, who had a little royal blood – being descended from Thomas, the first Duke of Gloucester, son of Edward III. – and he bethought himself that, now all the House of Lancaster was gone, and so many of the House of York, he might possibly become king. But he had hardly begun to make a plot, before the keen-sighted, watchful Richard found it out, and had him seized and beheaded.

There was another plot, though, that Richard did not find out in time. The real House of Lancaster had ended when poor young Edward was killed at Tewkesbury; but the Beauforts – the children of that younger family of John of Gaunt, who had first begun the quarrel with the Duke of York – were not all dead. Lady Margaret Beaufort, the daughter of the eldest son, had married a Welsh gentleman named Edmund Tudor, and had a son called Henry Tudor, Earl of Richmond. Edward IV. had always feared that this youth might rise against him, and he had been obliged to wander about in France and Brittany since the death of his father; but nobody was afraid of Lady Margaret, and she had married a Yorkist nobleman, Lord Stanley.

Now, the eldest daughter of Edward IV. – Elizabeth, or Lady Bessee, as she was called – was older than her poor young brothers; and she heard, to her great horror, that her uncle wanted to commit the great wickedness of making her his wife, after poor Anne Nevil's death. There is a curious old set of verses, written by Lord Stanley's squire, which says that Lady Bessee called Lord Stanley to a secret room, and begged him to send to his stepson, Richmond, to invite him to come to England and set them all free.

Stanley said he could not write well enough, and that he could not trust a scribe; but Lady Bessee said she could write as well as any scribe in England. So she told him to come to her chamber at nine that evening, with his trusty squire; and there she wrote letters, kneeling by the table, to all the noblemen likely to be discontented with Richard, and appointing a place of meeting with Stanley; and she promised herself that, if Henry Tudor would come and overthrow the cruel tyrant Richard, she would marry him: and she sent him a ring in pledge of her promise.

Henry was in Brittany when he received the letter. He kissed the ring, but waited long before he made up his mind to try his fortune. At last he sailed in a French ship, and landed at Milford Haven – for he knew the Welsh would be delighted to see him;

and, as he was really descended from the great British chiefs, they seemed to think that to make him king of England would be almost like having King Arthur back again.

They gathered round him, and so did a great many English nobles and gentlemen. But Richard, though very angry, was not much alarmed, for he knew Henry Tudor had never seen a battle. He marched out to meet him, and a terrible fight took place at Redmore Heath, near Market Bosworth, where, after long and desperate struggling, Richard was overwhelmed and slain, his banner taken, and his men either killed or driven from the field. His body was found gashed, bleeding, and stripped; and thus was thrown across a horse and carried into Leicester, where he had slept the night before.

The crown he had worn over his helmet was picked up from the branches of a hawthorn, and set on the head of Henry Tudor. Richard was the last king of the Plantagenet family, who had ruled over England for more than three hundred years. This battle of Bosworth likewise finished the whole bloody war of the Red and White Roses.

CHAPTER XXV.

HENRY VII. A.D. 1485 – 1509.

Henry Tudor married the Lady Bessee as soon as he came to London, and by this marriage the causes of the Red and white Roses were united; so that he took for his badge a great rose – half red and half white. You may see it carved all over the beautiful chapel that he built on to Westminster Abbey to be buried in.

He was not a very pleasant person; he was stiff, and cold, and dry, and very mean and covetous in some ways – though he liked to make a grand show, and dress all his court in cloth of gold and silver, and the very horses in velvet housings, whenever there was any state occasion. Nobody greatly cared for him; but the whole country was so worn out with the troubles of the Wars of the Roses, that there was no desire to interfere with him; and people only grumbled, and said he did not treat his gentle, beautiful wife Elizabeth as he ought to do, but was jealous of her being a king's daughter. There was one person who did hate him most bitterly, and that was the Duchess of Burgundy, the sister of Edward IV. and Richard III.: the same who, as I told you, encouraged printing so much. She felt as if a mean upstart had got into the place of her brothers, and his having married her niece did not make it seem a bit the better to her. There was one nephew left – the poor young orphan son of George, Duke of Clarence – but he had always been quite silly, and Henry VII. had him watched carefully, for fear some one should set him up to claim the crown. He was called Earl of Warwick, as heir to his grandfather, the king-maker.

Suddenly, a young man came to Ireland and pretended to be this Earl of Warwick. He deceived a good many of the Irish, and the Mayor of Dublin actually took him to St. Patrick's Cathedral, where he was crowned as King Edward the Sixth: and then he was carried to the banquet upon an Irish chieftain's back. He came to England with some Irish followers, and some German soldiers hired by the duchess; and a few, but not many, English joined him. Henry met him at a village called Stoke, near Newark, and all his Germans and Irish were killed, and he himself made prisoner. Then he confessed that he was really a baker's son named Lambert Simnel; and, as he turned out to be a poor weak lad, whom designing people had made to do just what they pleased, the king took him into his kitchen as a scullion; and, as he behaved well there, afterwards set him to look after the falcons, that people used to keep to go out with to catch partridges and herons.

But after this, a young man appeared under the protection of the Duchess of Burgundy, who said he was no other than the poor little Duke of York, Richard, who had escaped from the Tower when his brother was murdered. Englishmen, who came from Flanders, said that he was a clever, cowardly lad of the name of Peter (or Perkin) Warbeck, the son of a townsman of Tournay; but the duchess persuaded King James IV. of Scotland to believe him a real royal Plantagenet. He went to Edinburgh, married a beautiful lady, cousin to the king, and James led him into England at the head of an army to put forward his claim. But nobody would join him, and the Scots did not care about him; so James sent him away to Ireland, whence he went to Cornwall. However, he soon found fighting was of no use, and fled away to the New Forest, where he was taken prisoner. He was set in the stocks, and there made to confess that he was really Perkin Warbeck and no duke, and then he was shut up in the Tower. But there he made friends with the real Earl of Warwick, and persuaded him into a plan for escape; but this was found out, and Henry, thinking that he should never have any peace or safety whilst either of them was alive, caused Perkin to be hanged, and poor innocent Edward of Warwick to be beheaded.

It was thought that this cruel deed was done because Henry found that foreign kings did not think him safe upon the throne while one Plantagenet was left alive, and would not give their children in marriage to his sons and daughters. He was very anxious to make grand marriages for his children, and make peace with Scotland by a wedding between King James and his eldest daughter, Margaret. For his eldest son, Arthur, Prince of Wales, he obtained Katharine, the daughter of the King of Aragon and Queen of Castille, and she was brought to England while both were mere children. Prince Arthur died when only eighteen years old; and King Henry then said that they had been both such children that they could not be considered really married, and so that Katharine had better marry his next son, Henry, although everyone knew that no marriage between a man and his brother's widow could be lawful. The truth was that he did not like to give up all the money and jewels she had brought; and the matter remained in dispute for some years – nor was it settled when King Henry himself died, after an illness that no one expected would cause his death. Nobody was very sorry for him, for he had been hard upon everyone, and had encouraged two wicked judges, named Dudley and Empson, who made people pay most unjust demands,

demands, and did everything to fill the king's treasury and make themselves rich at the same time.

It was a time when many changes were going on peacefully. The great nobles had grown much poorer and less powerful; and the country squires and chief people in the towns reckoned for much more in the State. Moreover, there was much learning and study going on everywhere. Greek began to be taught as well as Latin, and the New Testament was thus read in the language in which the apostles themselves wrote; and that led people to think over some of the evil ways that had grown up in their churches and abbeys, during those long, grievous years, when no one thought of much but fighting, or of getting out of the way of the enemy.

The king himself, and all his family, loved learning, and nobody more than his son Henry, who – if his elder brother had lived – was to have been archbishop of Canterbury.

It was in this reign, too, that America was discovered – though not by the English, but by Christopher Columbus, an Italian, who came out in ships that were lent to him by Isabel, the Queen of Spain, mother to Katharine, Princess of Wales. Henry had been very near sending Columbus, only he did not like spending so much money. How ever, he afterwards did send out some ships, which discovered Newfoundland. Henry died in the year 1509.

CHAPTER XXVI.

HENRY VIII. AND CARDINAL WOLSEY. A.D. 1509 – 1529.

The new king was very fond of the Princess Katharine, and he married her soon after his father's death, without asking any more questions about the right or wrong of it. He began with very gallant and prosperous times. He was very handsome, and skilled in all sports and games, and had such frank, free manners, that the people felt as if they had one of their best old Plantagenets back again. They were pleased, too, when he quarreled with the King of France, and like an old Plantagenet, led an army across the sea and besieged the town of Tournay. Again, it was like the time of Edward III., for James IV. of Scotland was a friend of the French king, and came across the Border with all the strength of Scotland, to ravage England while Henry was away. But there were plenty of stout Englishmen left, and under the Earl of Surrey, they beat the Scots entirely at the battle of Flodden field; and King James himself was not taken, but left dead upon the field, while his kingdom went to his poor little baby son. Though there had been a battle in France it was not another Crecy, for the French ran away so fast that it was called the battle of the Spurs. However, Henry's expedition did not come to much, for he did not get all the help he was promised; and he made peace with the French king, giving him in marriage his beautiful young sister Mary – though King Louis was an old, helpless, sickly man. Indeed, he only lived six weeks after the wedding, and before there was time to fetch Queen Mary home again, she had married a gentleman named Charles Brandon. She told he brother that she had married once to please him, and now she had married to please herself. But he forgave her, and made her husband Duke of Suffolk.

Henry's chief adviser, at this time, was Thomas Wolsey, Archbishop of York; a very able man, and of most splendid tastes and habits – outdoing even the Tudors in love of show. The pope had made him a cardinal – that is, one of the clergy, who are counted as parish priests in the diocese of Rome, and therefore have a right to choose the pope. They wear scarlet hats, capes, and shoes, and are the highest rank of all the clergy except the pope. Indeed, Cardinal Wolsey was in hopes of being chosen pope himself, and setting the whole Church to rights – for there had been several very wicked men reigning at Rome, one after the other, and they had brought things to such a pass that everyone felt there would be some great judgment from God if some improvement were not made. Most of Wolsey's arrangements with foreign princes had this end in view. The new king of France, Francis I., was young, brilliant and splendid, like Henry, and the two had a conference near Calais, when they brought their queens and their whole Court, and put up tents of velvet, silk, and gold – while everything was so extraordinarily magnificent, that the meeting has ever since been called the Field of the Cloth of Gold.

However, nothing came of it all. Cardinal Wolsey thought Francis's enemy – the Emperor Charles V. – more likely to help him to be pope, and make his master go over to that side; but after all an Italian was chosen in his stead. And there came a new trouble in his way. The king and queen had been married a good many years, and they had only one child alive, and that was a girl, the Lady Mary - all the others had died as soon as they were born - and statesmen began to think that if there never was a son at all, there might be fresh wars when Henry died; while others said that the loss of the children was to punish them for marrying unlawfully. Wolsey himself began to wish that the pope would say that it had never been a real marriage, and so to set the king free to put Katharine away and take another wife - some grand princess abroad. This was thinking more of what seemed prudent than of the right; and it turned out ill for Wolsey and all besides, for no sooner had the notion of setting aside poor Katharine come into his mind, than the king cast his eyes on Anne Boleyn, one of her maids of honor - a lively lady, who had been to France with his sister Mary. He was bent on marrying her, and insisted on the pope's giving sentence against Katharine. But the pope would not make any answer at all; first, because he was enquiring, and then because he could not well offend Katharine's nephew, the Emperor. Time went on, and the king grew more impatient, and at last a clergyman, named Thomas Cranmer, said that he might settle the matter by asking the learned men at the universities whether it was lawful for a man to marry his brother's widow. "He has got the right sow by the ear," cried Henry, who was not choice in his words, and he determined that the universities should decide it. But Wolsey would not help the king here. He knew that the pope had been the only person to decide such questions all over the Western Church for many centuries; and, besides, he had never intended to assist the king to lower himself by taking a wife like Anne Boleyn. But his secretary, Thomas Crumwell, told the king all of Wolsey's disapproval, and between them they found out something that the cardinal had done by the king's own wish, but which did not agree with the old disused laws. He was put down from all his offices of state, and accused of treason against the king; but while he was being brought to London to be tried, he became so ill at the abbey at Leicester that he was forced to remain there, and in a few days he died, saying, sadly – "If I had served God as I have served my king, He would not have forsaken me in my old age."

With Cardinal Wolsey ended the first twenty years of Henry's reign, and all that had ever been good in it.

CHAPTER XXVII.

HENRY VIII. AND HIS WIVES. A.D. 1528 – 1547.

When Henry VIII. had so ungratefully treated Cardinal Wolsey, there was no one to keep him in order. He would have no more to do with the pope, but said he was head of the Church of England himself, and could settle matters his own way. He really was a very learned man, and had written a book to uphold the doctrines of the Church, which had caused the people to call him the Defender of the Faith. After the king's or queen's name on an English coin you may see F.D. – *Fidei Defensor*. This stands for that name in Latin. But Henry used his learning now against the pope. He declared that his marriage with Katharine was good for nothing, and sent her away to a house in Huntingdonshire, where, in three years' time, she pined away and died. In the meantime, he had married Anne Boleyn, taken Crumwell for his chief adviser, and had made Thomas Cranmer archbishop of Canterbury. Then, calling himself the head of the Church, he insisted that all his people should own him as such; but the good ones knew that our Lord Jesus Christ is the only real Head of the Church, and they had learnt to believe that the pope is the father bishop of the west, though he had sometimes taken more power than he ought, and no king could ever be the same as a patriarch or father bishop. So they refused, and Henry cut off the heads of two of the best – Bishop Fisher and Sir Thomas More – though they had been his great friends. Sir Thomas More's good daughter Margaret, came and kissed him on his way to be executed; and afterwards, when his head was placed on a spike on London Bridge, she came by night in a boat and took it home in her arms.

There were many people, however, who were glad to break with the pope, because so much had gone amiss in the Church, and they wanted to set it to rights. There was so much more reading, now that printing had been invented, that many could read who had never learnt Latin, and so a translation of the Bible was to be made for them, and there was a great desire that the Church Services – many of which had also been in Latin – should likewise be put into English, and the litany was first translated, but no more at present. The king and Crumwell had taken it upon them to go on with what had been begun in Wolsey's time – the looking into the state of all the monasteries. Some were found going on badly, and the messengers took care to make the worst of everything. So all the worst houses were broken up, and the monks sent to their homes, with a small payment to maintain them for the rest of their lives.

As to the lands that good men of old had given to keep up the convents, that God might be praised there, Henry made gifts of them to the lords about Court. Whoever chose to ask for an abbey could get it, from the king's good nature; and, as they wanted more and more, Henry went on breaking up the monasteries, till the whole of them were gone. A good deal of their riches he kept for himself, and two new bishoprics were endowed from their spoils, but most of them were bestowed on the courtiers. The king, however, did not at all intend to change the teaching of the Church, and whenever a person was detected in teaching any thing contrary to her doctrines, as they were at the time understood, he was tried by a court of clergymen and lawyers before the bishop, and, if convicted, was – according to the cruel custom of those times – burnt to death at a stake in the market place of the next town.

Meantime, the new queen, Anne Boleyn, whom the king had married privately in May, 1533, had not prospered. She had one little daughter, named Elizabeth, and a son, who died; and then the king began to admire one of her ladies, named Jane Seymour. Seeing this Anne's enemies either invented stories against her, or made the worst of some foolish, unlady-like, and unqueen-like things she had said and done, so that the king thought she wished for his death. She was accused of high treason, sentenced to death, and beheaded: thus paying a heavy price for the harm she had done good Queen Katharine.

The king, directly after, married Jane Seymour; but she lived only a very short time, dying immediately after the christening of her first son, who was named Edward.

Then the king was persuaded by Lord Crumwell to marry a foreign princess called Anne of Cleves. A great painter was sent to bring her picture, and made her very beautiful in it; but when she arrived, she proved to be not only plain-featured but large and clumsy, and the king could not bear the sight of her, and said they had sent him a great Flanders mare by way of queen. So he made Cranmer find some foolish excuse for breaking this marriage also, and was so angry with Thomas Crumwell for having led him into it, that this favorite was in turn thrown into prison and beheaded.

The king chose another English wife, named Katharine Howard; but, after he had married her, it was found out that she had been very ill brought up, and the bad people with whom she had been left came and accused her of the evil into which they had led her. So the king cut off her head, likewise, and then

then wanted to find another wife; but no foreign princess would take a husband who had put away two wives and beheaded two more, and one Italian lady actually answered that she was much obliged to him, but she could not venture to marry him, because she had only one neck.

At last he found an English widow, Lady Latimer, whose maiden name was Katharine Parr, and married her. He was diseased now, lame with gout, and very large and fat; and she nursed him kindly, and being a good-natured woman, persuaded him to be kinder to his daughters, Mary and Elizabeth, than he had ever been since the disgrace of their mothers; and she did her best to keep him in good humor, but he went on doing cruel things, even to the end of his life; and, at the very last, had in prison the very same Duke of Norfolk who had won the battle of Flodden, and would have put him to death in a few days' time, only that his own death prevented it.

Yet, strange to say, Henry VIII. was not hated as might have been expected. His cruelties were chiefly to the nobles, not to the common people; and he would do good-natured things, and speak with a frank, open manner, that was much liked. England was prosperous, too, and shopkeepers, farmers, and all were well off; there was plenty of bread and meat for all, and the foreign nations were afraid to go to war with us. So the English people, on the whole, loved "Bluff King Hal," as they called him, and did not think much about his many wickednesses, or care how many heads he cut off. He died in the year 1547. The changes in his time are generally called the beginning of the Reformation.

CHAPTER XXVIII.

EDWARD VI. A.D. 1547 – 1553.

The little son of Henry VIII. and Jane Seymour of course reigned after him as Edward VI. He was a quiet, gentle boy exceedingly fond of learning and study, and there were great expectations of him; but, as he was only nine years old, the affairs of state were managed by his council.

The chief of the council were his two uncles – his mother's brothers, Edward and Thomas Seymour, the elder of whom had been made Duke of Somerset – together with Archbishop Cranmer; but it was not long before the duke quarreled with his brother Thomas, put him into the Tower, and cut off his head, so that it seemed as if the days of Henry VIII. were not yet over.

The Duke of Somerset and Archbishop Cranmer wanted to make many more changes in the Church of England than Henry VIII. had ever allowed. They had all the Prayer-book Services translated into English, leaving out such parts as they did not approve; The Lessons were read from the English Bible, and people were greatly delighted at being able to worship and to listen to God's Word in their own tongue. The first day on which the English Prayer-book was used was the Whitsunday of 1548. The Bibles were chained to the desks as being so precious and valuable; and crowds would stand, or sit, and listen for hours together to any one who would read to them, without caring if he were a clergyman or not; and men who tried to explain, without being properly taught, often made great mistakes.

Indeed, in Germany and France a great deal of the same kind had been going on for some time past, though not with any sort of leave from the kings or bishops, as there was in England, and thus the reformers there broke quite off from the Church, and fancied they could do without bishops. This great break was called the Reformation, because it professed to set matters of religion to rights; and in Germany the reformers called themselves Protestants, because they protested some of the teachings of the Church of Rome.

Cranmer had at one time been in Germany, and had made friends with some of these German and Swiss Protestants, and he invited them to England to consult and help him and his friends. Several of them came, and they found fault with our old English Prayer-book – though it had never been the same as the Roman one – and it was altered again to please them and their friends, and brought out as King Edward's second book. Indeed, they tried to persuade the English to be like themselves – with very few services, no ornaments in the churches, and no bishops; and things seemed to be tending more and more to what they desired, for the king was too young not to do what his tutors and governors wished, and his uncle and Cranmer were all on their side.

However, there was another great nobleman, the Duke of Northumberland, who wanted to be as powerful as the Duke of Somerset. He was the son of Dudley, the wicked judge under Henry VII., who had made himself so rich, and he managed to take advantage of the people being discontented with Somerset to get the king into his own hands, accuse Somerset of treason, send him to the Tower, and cut off his head.

The king at this time was sixteen. He had never been strong, and he had learnt and worked much more than was good for him. He wrote a journal, and though he never says he grieved for his uncles, most likely he did, for he had few near him who really loved or cared for him, and he was fast falling into decline, so that it became quite plain that he was not likely ever to be a grown-up king. There was a great difficulty as to who was to reign after him. The natural person would have been his eldest sister, Mary, but King Henry had forbidden her and Elizabeth to be spoken of as princesses or heiresses of the crown; and, besides, Mary held so firmly to the Church, as she had learnt to believe in it in her youth, that the reformers knew she would undo all their work.

There was a little Scottish girl, also named Mary – the grand-daughter of Margaret, eldest daughter of Henry VII. Poor child, she had been a queen from babyhood, for her father had died of grief when she was but a week old; and there had been some notion of marrying her to King Edward, and so ending the wars, but the Scots did not like this, and sent her away to be married to the Dauphin, Francois, eldest son of the king of France. If Edward's sisters were not to reign, she came next; but the English would not have borne to be joined on to the French; and there were the grand-daughters of Mary, that other sister of Henry VIII., who were thorough Englishwomen. Lady Jane Grey, the eldest of them, was a good, sweet, pious, and diligent girl of fifteen, wonderfully learned. But it was not for that reason, only for the sake of the royal blood, that the Duke of Northumberland asked her in marriage for his son, Guildford Dudley. When they were married, the duke and Cranmer began to persuade the poor, sick, young king that it was his duty to leave his crown away from his sister Mary to Lady Jane, who would go on with the Reformation, while Mary would try to overthrow it. In truth, young Edward had not right to will away the crown; but he was only sixteen, and could only trust to what the archbishop and his council told him. So he signed the parchment they brought him, and after that he quickly grew worse.

The people grew afraid that Northumberland was shutting him up and misusing him, and once he came to the window of his palace and looked out at them, to show he was alive; but he died only a fortnight later, and we cannot guess what he would have been when he was grown up.

CHAPTER XXIX.

MARY I. A.D. 1553 – 1588.

The Duke of Northumberland kept king Edward's death a secret till he had proclaimed Jane queen of England. The poor girl knew that a great wrong was being done in her name. She wept bitterly, and begged that she might not be forced to accept the crown; but she could do nothing to prevent it, when her father and husband, and his father, all were bent on making her obey them; and so she had to sit as a queen in the royal apartments in the Tower of London.

But as soon as the news reached Mary, she set off riding towards London; and, as everyone knew her to be the right queen, and no one would be tricked by Dudley, the whole of the people joined her, and even Northumberland was obliged to throw up his hat and cry "God save Queen Mary." Jane and her husband were safely kept, but Mary meant no harm by them if their friends would have been quiet. However, the people became discontented when Mary began to have the Latin service used again, and put Archbishop Cranmer in prison for having favored Jane. She showed in every way that she thought all her brother's advisers had done very wrong. She wanted to be under the Pope again, and she engaged herself to marry the King of Spain, her cousin, Philip II. This was very foolish of her, for she was a middle-aged woman, pale, and low-spirited; and he was much younger, and of a silent, gloomy temper, so that everyone was afraid of him. All her best friends advised her not, and the English hated the notion so much, that the little children played at the queen's wedding in their games, and always ended by pretending to hang the King of Spain. Northumberland thought this discontent gave another chance for his plan, and tried to raise the people in favor of Jane; but so few joined him that Mary very soon put them down, and beheaded Northumberland. She thought, too, that the quiet of the country would never be secure while Jane lived, and so she consented to her being put to death. Jane behaved with beautiful firmness and patience. Her husband was led out first and beheaded, and then she followed. She was most good and innocent in herself, and it was for the faults of others that she suffered. Mary's sister Elizabeth, was suspected, and sent to the Tower. She came in a boat on the Thames to the Traitor's Gate; but, when she found where she was, she sat down on the stone steps and said, "This is a place for traitors, and I am none." After a time she was allowed to live in the country, but closely watched.

Philip of Spain came and was married to Mary. She was very fond of him, but he was not very kind to her, and he had too much to do in his other kingdoms to spend much time with her, so that she was always pining after him. Her great wish in choosing him was to be helped in bringing the country back to the old obedience to the Pope; and she succeeded in having the English Church reconciled, and received again to communion with Rome. The new service she would under no consideration have established in her house. This displeased many of her subjects exceedingly. They thought they should be forbidden to read the Bible – they could not endure the Latin service – and those who had been taught by the foreigners fancied that all proper reverence and beauty in church was a sort of idolatry. Some fled away into Holland and

Germany, and others, who staid, and taught loudly against the doctrines that were to be brought back again, were seized and thrown into prison.

Those bishops who had been foremost in the changes of course were the first to be tried for their teaching. The punishment was the dreadful one of being burnt alive, chained to a stake. Bishop Hooper died in this way at Gloucester, and Bishop Ridley and Bishop Latimer were both burnt at the same time at Oxford, encouraging one another to die bravely as martyrs for the truth, as they held it. Cranmer was in prison already for supporting Jane Grey, and he was condemned to death; but he was led to expect that he would be spared the fire if he would allow that the old faith, as Rome held it, was the right one. Paper after paper was brought, such as would please the queen and his judges, and he signed them all; but after all, it turned out that none would do, and that he was to be burnt in spite of them. The he felt what a base part he had acted, and was ashamed when he thought how bravely his brethren had died on the same spot: and when he was chained to the stake and the fire lighted, he held his right hand over the flame to be burnt first, because it had signed what he did not really believe, and he cried out, "This unworthy hand!"

Altogether, about three hundred people were burnt in Queen Mary's reign for denying one or other of the doctrines that the Pope thought the right ones. It was a terrible time; and the queen, who had only longed to do right and restore her country to the Church, found herself hated and disliked by everyone. Even the Pope, who had a quarrel with her husband, did not treat her warmly; and the nobles, who had taken possession of the abbey lands, were determined never to let her restore them. Her husband did not love her, or like England. However, he persuaded her to help him in a war with the French, with which England out to have had nothing to do, and the consequence was that a brave French duke took the city of Calais, the very last possession of the English in France. Mary was so exceedingly grieved, that she said that when she died the name of Calais would be found written on her heart.

She was already ill, and there was a bad fever at the time, of which many of those she most loved and trusted had fallen sick. She died, in 1558, a melancholy and sorrowful woman, after reigning only five years.

CHAPTER XXX.

ELIZABETH. A.D. 1558 – 1587.

All through Queen Mary's time, her sister Elizabeth, Anne Boleyn's daughter, had been in trouble. Those who held by Queen Mary, and maintained Henry's first marriage, said that his wedding with Anne was no real one, and so that Elizabeth ought not to reign; but then there was no one else to take in her stead, except the young Queen Mary of Scotland, wife to the French dauphin. All who wished for the Reformation, and dreaded Mary's persecutions had hoped to see Elizabeth queen, and this had made Mary much afraid of her; and she was so closely watched and guarded that once she even said she wished she was a milkmaid, to be left in peace. While she had been in the Tower she had made friends with another prisoner, Robert Dudley, brother to the husband of Lady Jane Grey, and she continued to like him better than any other person as long as he lived.

When Mary died, Elizabeth was twenty-five, and the English were mostly willing to have her for their queen. She had read, thought, and learnt a great deal; and she took care to have the advice of wise men, especially of the great Thomas Cecil, whom she made Lord Burleigh, and kept as her adviser as long as he lived. She did not always follow even his advice, however; but, whenever she did, it was the better for her. She knew Robert Dudley was not wise, so, though she was so fond of him, she never let him manage her affairs for her. She would have wished to marry, but she knew her subjects would think this disgraceful, so she only made him Earl of Leicester: and her liking for him prevented her from ever bringing herself to accept any of the foreign princes who were always making proposals to her. Unfortunately he was not a good man, and did not make a good use of her favor, and he was much disliked by all the queen's best friends.

She was very fond of making stately journeys through the country. All the poor people ran to see her and admire her; but the noblemen who had to entertain her were almost ruined, she brought so many people who ate so much, and she expected such presents. These journeys were called Progresses. The most famous was to Lord Leicester's castle of Kenilworth, but he could quite afford it. He kept the clock's hands at twelve o'clock all the time, that it might always seem to be dinner time!

Elizabeth wanted to keep the English Church a pure and true branch of the Church, free of the mistakes that had crept in before her father's time. So she restored the English Prayer-book, and cancelled all that Mary had done; the people who had gone into exile returned, and all the Protestants abroad reckoned her as on their side. But, on the other hand, the Pope would not regard her as queen at all, and cut her and her country off from the Church, while Mary of Scotland and her husband called themselves the true queen and king of England; and such of the English as believed the Pope to have the first right over the Church, held with him and Mary of Scotland. They were called Roman Catholics, while Elizabeth and her friends were the real Catholics, for they held with the Church Universal of old: and it was the Pope who had broken off with them for not accepting his doctrines, not they with the Pope. The English who had lived abroad in Mary's time wanted to have much more altered, and to have churches and services much less beautiful and more plain than they were. But Elizabeth never would consent to this; and these people called themselves Puritans, and continued to object to the Episcopal form of worship.

Mary of Scotland was two years queen of France, and then her husband died, and she had to come back to Scotland. There most of the people had taken up the doctrines that made them hate the sight of the clergy and services she had brought home from France; they called her an idolater, and would hardly bear that she should hear the old service in her own chapel. She was one of the most beautiful and charming women who ever lived, and if she had been as true and good as she was lovely, nobody could have done more good; but the court of France at that time was a wicked place, and she had learnt much of the wickedness. She married a young nobleman named Henry Stuart, a cousin of her own, but he turned out foolish, selfish and head-strong, and made her miserable; indeed, he helped to kill her secretary in her own bedroom before her eyes. She hated him so much at last, that there is only too much reason to fear that she knew of the plot, laid by some of her lords, to blow the poor man's house up with gunpowder, while he lay is his bed ill of smallpox. At any rate, she very soon married one of the very worst of the nobles who had committed the murder. Her subjects could not bear this, and they rose against her and made her prisoner, while her husband fled the country. They shut her up in a castle in the middle of a lake, and obliged her to give up her crown to her little son, James VI. - a baby not a year old. However, her sweet words persuaded a boy who waited on her to steal the keys, and row her across the lake, and she was soon at the head of an army of her Roman Catholic subjects. They were defeated, however, and she found no place safe for her in Scotland, so she fled across the Border to England. Queen Elizabeth hardly knew what to do. She believed that Mary had really had to do with Henry Stuart's death, but she could not bear to make such a crime known in a cousin and queen; and what made it all more difficult to judge was, that the kings of France and Spain, and all the Roman Catholics at home, thought Mary ought to be queen instead of Elizabeth, and she might have been set up against England if she might had gone abroad, or been left at large, while in Scotland she would have been murdered. The end of it was that Elizabeth kept her shut up in different castles. There she managed to interest the English Roman Catholics in her, and get them to lay plots, which always were found out. Then nobles were put to death, and Mary was more closely watched. This went on for nineteen years, and at last a worse plot than all was found out – for actually killing Queen Elizabeth. Her servants did not act honorably, for when they found out what was going on they pretended not to know, so that Mary might go on writing worse and worse things, and then, at last, the whole was made known. Mary was tried and sentenced to death, but Elizabeth was a long time making up her mind to sign the order for her execution, and at last punished the clerks who sent it off, as if it had been their fault.

So Queen Mary of Scotland was beheaded at Fotheringay Castle, showing much bravery and piety. There are many people who still believe that she was really innocent of all that she was accused of, and that she only was ruined by the plots that were laid against her.

CHAPTER XXXI.

ELIZABETH'S REIGN. A.D. 1587 – 1602.

No reign ever was more glorious or better for the people than Queen Elizabeth's. It was a time when there were many very great men living – soldiers, sailors, writers, poets – and they all loved and look up to the queen as the mother of her country. There really was nothing she did love like the good of her people, and somehow they all felt and knew it, and "Good Queen Bess" had their hearts – though she was not always right, and had some serious faults.

The worst of her faults was not telling the truth. Somehow kings and rulers had, at that time, learnt to believe that when they were dealing with other countries anything was fair, and that it was not wrong to tell falsehoods to hide a secret, nor to make promises they never meant to keep. People used to do so who would never have told a lie on their own account to their neighbor, and Lord Burleigh and Queen Elizabeth did so very often, and often behaved meanly and shabbily to people who had trusted to their promises. Her other fault was vanity. She was a little woman, with bright eyes, and rather hooked nose, and sandy hair, but she managed to look every inch a queen, and her eye, when displeased, was like a lion's. She had really been in love with Lord Leicester, and every now and then he hoped she would marry him; indeed, there is reason to fear that he had his wife secretly killed, in order that he might be able to wed the queen; but she saw that the people would not allow her to do so, and gave it up. But she liked to be courted. She allowed foreign princes to send her their portraits, rings, and jewels, and sometimes to come and see her, but she never made up her mind to take them. And as to the gentlemen at her own court, she liked them to make the most absurd and ridiculous compliments to her, calling her their sun and goddess, and her hair golden beams of the morning, and the like; and the older she grew the more of these fine speeches she required of them. Her dress – a huge hoop, a tall ruff all over lace, and jewels in the utmost profusion – was as splendid as it could be made, and in wonderful variety. She is said to have had three hundred gowns and thirty wigs. Lord Burleigh said of her that she was sometimes more than a man, and sometimes less than a woman. And so she was, when she did not like her ladies to wear handsome dresses.

One of the people who had wanted to marry her was her brother-in-law, Philip of Spain, but she was far too wise, and he and she were bitter enemies all the rest of their lives. His subjects in Holland had become Protestants, and he persecuted them so harshly that they broke away from him. They wanted Elizabeth to be their queen, but she would not, though she sent Lord Leicester to help them with an army. With him went his nephew, Sir Philip Sydney, the most good, and learned, and graceful gentleman at court. There was great grief when Sir Philip was struck by a cannon ball in the thigh, and died after nine days pain. It was as he was being carried from the field, faint and thirsty, that some one had just brought him a cup of water, when he saw a poor soldier, worse hurt than himself, looking at it with longing eyes. He put it from him untasted, and said, "Take it, thy necessity is greater than mine."

After the execution of Mary of Scotland, Philip of Spain resolved to punish Elizabeth and the English, and force them back to obedience to the pope. He fitted out an immense fleet, and filled it with fighting men. So strong was it that, as armada is the Spanish for a fleet, it was called the Invincible Armada. It sailed for England, the men expecting to burn and ruin all before them. But the English ships were ready. Little as they were, they hunted and tormented the big Spaniards all the way up the English Channel; and, just as the Armada had passed the Straits of Dover, there came on such dreadful storms that the ships were driven and broken before it, and wrecked all round the coasts – even in Scotland and Ireland – and very few ever reached home again. The English felt that God had protected them with His wind and storm, and had fought for them.

Lord Leicester died not long after, and the queen became almost equally fond of his stepson, the Earl of Essex, who was a brave, high-spirited young man, only too proud.

The sailors of Queen Elizabeth's time were some of the bravest and most skilful that ever lived. Sir Francis Drake sailed round the world in the good ship Pelican, and when he brought her into the Thames the queen went to look at her. Sir Walter Raleigh was another great sailor, and a most courtly gentleman besides. He took out the first English settlers to North America, and named their new home Virginia – after the virgin queen – and he brought home from South America our good friend the potato root; and, also he learnt their to smoke tobacco. The first time his servant saw this done in England, he thought his master must be on fire, and threw a bucket of water over him to put it out.

The queen valued these brave men much, but she

liked none so well as Lord Essex, till at last he displeased her, and she sent him to govern Ireland. There he fell into difficulties, and she wrote angry letters, which made him think his enemies were setting her against him. So he came back without leave; and one morning came straight into her dressing chamber, where she was sitting, with her thin grey hair being combed, before she put on one of her thirty wigs, or painted her face. She was very angry, and would not forgive him, and he got into a rage, too; and she heard he had said she was an old woman, crooked in temper as in person. What was far worse, he raised the Londoners to break out in a tumult to uphold him. He was taken and sent to the Tower, tried for treason, and found guilty of death. But the queen still loved him, and waited and waited for some message or token to ask her pardon. None came, and she thought he was too proud to beg for mercy. She signed the death warrant, and Essex died on the block. But soon she found that he had really sent a ring she once had given him, to a lady who was to show it to her, in token that he craved her pardon. The ring had been taken by mistake to a cruel lady who hated him, and kept it back. But by-and-by this lady was sick to death. Then she repented, and sent for the queen and gave her the ring, and confessed her wickedness. Poor Queen Elizabeth – her very heart was broken. She said to the dying woman, "God may forgive you, but I cannot." She said little more after that. She was old, and her strength failed her. Day after day she sat on a pile of cushions, with her finger on her lips, still growing weaker, and begging for the prayers the archbishop read her. And thus, she who had once been so great and spirited, sank into death, when seventy years old, in the year 1602.

CHAPTER XXXII.

JAMES I. A.D. 1602 – 1625.

After Queen Elizabeth's death, the next heir was James, the son of Mary of Scotland, and had reigned there ever since his mother had been driven away. He had been brought up very strictly by the Scottish Reformers, who had made him very learned, and kept him under great restraint; and all that he had undergone had tended to make him awkward and strange in his manners. He was timid, and could not bear to see a drawn sword; and he was so much afraid of being murdered, that he used to wear a dress padded and stuffed out all over with wool, which made him look even more clumsy than he was by nature.

The English did not much admire their new king, though it really was a great blessing that England and Scotland should be under the same king at last, so as to end all the long and bloody wars that had gone on for so many years. Still, the Puritans thought that, as James had been brought up in their way of thinking, they would be allowed to make all the changes that Queen Elizabeth had stopped; and the Roman Catholics recollected that he was Queen Mary's son, and that his Reformed tutors had not made his life very pleasant to him as a boy, so they had hopes from him.

But they both were wrong. James had really read and thought much, and was a much wiser man at the bottom than anyone would have thought who had seen his disagreeable ways, and heard his silly way of talking. He thought the English Church was much more in the right than either of them, and he only wished that things should go on the same in England, and that the Scots should be brought to have bishops, and to use the prayers that Christians had used from the very old times, instead of each minister praying out of his own head, as had become the custom. But though he could not change the ways of the Scots at once, he caused all the best scholars and clergymen in his kingdom to go to work to make the translation of the Bible as right and good as it could be.

Long before this was finished, however, some of the Roman Catholics had formed a conspiracy for getting rid of all the chief people in the kingdom; and so, as they hoped, bringing the rest back to the pope. There were good men among the Roman Catholics who knew such an act would be horrible; but there were some among them who had learnt to hate everyone that they did not reckon as of the right religion, and to believe that everything was right that was done for the cause of their Church. So these men agreed that on the day of the meeting of Parliament, when the king, with the queen and Prince of Wales, would all be meeting the lords and commons, they would blow the whole of them up with gunpowder; and, while the country was all in confusion, the king dead, and almost all his lords and the chief country squires, they would take the king's younger children – Elizabeth or Charles, who were both quite little – and bring one up as a Roman Catholic to govern England.

They hired some cellars under the Houses of Parliament, and stored them with barrels of gunpowder, hidden by faggots; and the time was nearly come, when one of the lords called Monteagle, received a letter that puzzled him very much, advising him not to attend the meeting of Parliament, since a sudden destruction, would come upon all who would there be present, and yet so that they would not know the doer of it. No one knows who wrote the letter, but most likely it was one of the gentlemen who had been asked to join in the plot, and, though he would not betray his friends, could not bear that Lord Monteagle should perish. Lord Monteagle took the letter to the council, and there, after puzzling over it and wondering if it were a joke, the king said gunpowder was a means of sudden destruction; and it was agreed that, at any rate, it would be safer to look into the vaults. A party was sent to search, and there they found all the powder ready prepared, and, moreover, a man with a lantern, one Guy Fawkes, who had undertaken to be the one to set fire to the train of gunpowder, hoping to escape before the explosion. However he was seized in time, and was forced to make confession. Most of the gentlemen concerned fled into the country, and shut themselves up in a fortified house; but there, strange to say, a barrel of gunpowder chanced to get lighted, and thus many were much hurt in the very way that meant to hurt others.

There was a great thanksgiving all over the country, and it became the custom that, on the 5th of November – the day when the gunpowder plot was to have taken effect – there should be bonfires and fireworks, and Guy Fawkes' figure burnt, but people are getting wiser now, and think it better not to keep up the memory old crimes and hatreds.

Henry, Prince of Wales, was a fine lad, fond of all that was good, but a little too apt to talk of wars, and of being like Henry V. He was very fond of ships and sailors, and delighted in watching the building of a grand vessel that was to take his sister Elizabeth across the sea, when she was to marry the Count Palatine of the Rhine. Before the wedding, however, Prince Henry fell suddenly ill and died.

King James was a fond of favorites as ever Elizabeth had been, though not of the same persons. One of the worst things he ever did was the keeping Sir Walter Raleigh in the Tower for many years, and a last cutting off his head. It was asserted that Sir Walter had tried, when first James came, to set up a lady named Arabella Stuart to be queen; but if he was to be punished for that, it ought to have been directly, instead of keeping the sentence hanging over his head for years. The truth was that Sir Walter had been a great enemy to the Spaniards, and James wanted to please them, for he wished his son Charles to marry the daughter of the King of Spain. Charles wanted to see her first, and set off for Spain, in disguise, with the Duke of Buckingham, who was his friend, and his father's greatest favorite. But when reached he Madrid, he found that the princesses were not allowed to speak to any gentleman, nor to show their faces; and though he climbed over a wall to speak to her when she was walking in the garden, an attendant begged him to go away, or all her train would be punished. Charles went back disappointed, and, on his way through Paris, saw Henrietta Maria, the bright-eyed sister of the King of France, and set his heart on marrying her.

Before this was settled, however, King James was seized with an ague and died, in the year 1625. He was the first king of the family of Stuart, and a very strange person he was – wonderfully learned and exceedingly conceited; indeed, he like nothing better than to be called the English Solomon. The worst of him was that, like Elizabeth, he thought kings and rulers might tell falsehoods and deceive. He called this kingcraft, and took this very bad sort of cunning for wisdom.

CHAPTER XXXIII.

CHARLES I. A.D. 1625 – 1649.

So many of the great nobles had been killed in the Wars of the Roses, that the barons had lost all that great strength and power they had gained when they made King John sign Magna Carta. The kings got the power instead; and all through the reigns of the five Tudors, the sovereign had very little to hinder him from doing exactly as he pleased. But, in the meantime, the country squires and the great merchants who sat in the House of Commons had been getting richer and stronger, and read and thought more. As long as Queen Elizabeth lived they were contented, for they loved her and were proud of her, and she knew how to manage them. She scolded them sometimes, but when she saw that she was really vexing them she always changed, and she had smiles and good words for them, so that she could really do what she pleased with them.

But James I. was a disagreeable man to have to do with; and, instead of trying to please them, he talked a great deal about his own power as king, and how they ought to obey him; so that they were angered, and began to read the laws, and wonder how much power properly belonged to him. Now, when he died, his son Charles was a much pleasanter person; he was a gentleman in all his looks and ways, and had none of his father's awkward, ungainly tricks and habits. He was good and earnest, too, and there was nothing to take offence at in himself; so for some years all went on quietly, and there seemed to be a great improvement. But several things were against him. His friend, the Duke of Buckingham, was a proud, selfish man, who affronted almost everyone, and made a bad use of the king's favor; and the people were also vexed that the king should marry a Roman Catholic princess, Henrietta Maria, who would not go to church with him, nor even let herself be crowned by an English archbishop.

You heard that, in Queen Elizabeth's time, there were Puritans who would have liked to have the Prayer-book much more altered, and who fancied that every pious rule of old times must be wrong. They did not like the cross in baptism, nor the ring in marriage; and they could not bear to see a clergyman in a surplice. In many churches they took their own way, and did just as they pleased. But under James and Charles matters changed. Dr. Laud, whom Charles had made archbishop of Canterbury, had all the churches visited, and insisted on the parishioners setting them in order; and if a clergyman would not wear a surplice, not make a cross on the baptized child's forehead, nor obey the other laws of the Prayer-book, he was punished.

The Puritans were greatly displeased. They fancied the king and Dr. Laud wanted to make them all Roman Catholics again; and a great many so hated these Church rules, that they took ship and went off to North America to found a colony, where they might set up their own religion as they liked it. Those who staid continued to murmur and struggle against Laud.

There was another great matter of displeasure, and that was the way in which the king raised money. The right way is that he should call his Parliament together, and the House of Commons should grant him what he wanted. But there were other means. One was that every place in England should be called on to pay so much for ship money. This had begun when King Alfred raised his fleet to keep off the Danes; but it had come not to be spent on ships at all, but only be money for the king to use. Another way that the kings had of getting money was from fines. People who committed some small offence, that did not come under the regular laws, were brought before the Council in a room at Westminster, that had a ceiling painted with stars – and so was called the Star Chamber – and there were sentenced, sometimes to pay heavy sums of money, sometimes to have their ears cut off. This Court of the Star Chamber had been begun in the days of Henry VII., and it is only a wonder that the English had borne it so long.

One thing Charles I. did that pleased his people, and that was sending help to the French Protestants, who were having their town of Rochelle besieged. But the English were not pleased that the command of the army was given to the duke of Buckingham, his proud, insolent favorite. but Buckingham never went. As he was going to embark at Portsmouth, he was stabbed to the heart by a man named Felton; nobody clearly knows why.

Charles did not get on much better even when Buckingham was dead. Whenever he called a Parliament, fault was always found with him and with the laws. Then he tried to do without a Parliament; and, as he, of course, needed money, the calls for ship money came oftener, and the fines in the Star Chamber became heavier, and more cases for them were hunted out. Then murmurs arose. Just then, too, he and Archbishop Laud were trying to make the Scots return to the Church, by giving them bishops and a Prayer-book. But the first time the Service was read in a church at Edinburgh, a fishwoman, named Jenny Geddes, jumped up in a rage and threw a three-legged stool at the clergyman's head. Some Scots fancied they were being brought back to Rome; others hated whatever was commanded in England. All these leagued together, and raised an army to resist the king; and he was obliged to call a Parliament once more, to get money enough to resist them.

CHAPTER XXXIV.

THE LONG PARLIAMENT. A.D. 1641 – 1649.

When Charles I. was obliged to call his Parliament, the House of Commons met, angered at the length of time that had passed since they had been called, and determined to use their opportunity. They speedily put an end both to the payment of ship money and to the Court of the Star Chamber; and they threw into prison the two among the king's friends whom they most disliked, namely, Archbishop Laud and the Earl of Strafford. The earl had been governor of Ireland, and had kept great order there, but severely; and he thought that the king was the only person who ought to have any power, and was always advising the king to put down all resistance by the strong hand. He was thought a hard man, and very much hated; and when he was tried the Houses of Parliament gave sentence against him that he should be beheaded. Still, this could not be done without the king's warrant; and Charles at first stood out against giving up his faithful friend. But there was a great tumult, and the queen and her mother grew frightened, and entreated the king to save himself by giving up Lord Strafford, until at last he consented, and signed the paper ordering the execution. It was a sad act of weakness and cowardice, and he mourned over it all the days of his life.

The Parliament only asked more and more, and at last the king thought he must put a check on them. So he resolved to go down to the House and cause the five members who spoke against his power to be taken prisoners in his own presence. But he told his wife what he intended, and Henrietta Maria was so foolish

foolish as to tell Lady Carlisle, one of her ladies, and she sent warning to the five gentlemen, so that they were not in the House when Charles arrived; and the Londoners rose up in a great mob, and showed themselves so angry with him, that he took the queen and his children away into the country. The queen took her daughter Mary to Holland to marry the Prince of Orange; and there she bought muskets and gunpowder for her husband's army – for things had come to pass now that a civil war began. A civil war is the worst of all wars, for it is one between the people of the same country. England had had two civil wars before. There were the Barons' wars, between Henry III. and Simon de Montfort, about the keeping of Magna Carta; and there were the wars of the Roses, to settle whether York or Lancaster should reign. This war between Charles I. and the Parliament was to decide whether the king or the House of Commons should be most powerful. Those who held with the king called themselves Cavaliers, but the friends of the Parliament called them Malignants; and they in turn nicknamed the Parliamentary party Roundheads, because they often chose not to wear their hair in the prevailing fashion, long and flowing on their shoulders, but cut short round their heads. Most of the Roundheads were Puritans, and hated the Prayerbook, and all the strict rules for religious worship that Archbishop Laud had brought in; and the Cavaliers, on the other hand, held by the bishops and the Prayerbook. Some of the Cavaliers were very good men indeed, and led holy and Christian lives, like their master the king, but there were others who were only bold, dashing men, careless and full of mirth and mischief; and the Puritans were apt to think all amusements and pleasures wrong, so that they made out the

Cavaliers worse than they really were.

I do not think you would understand about all the battles, so I shall only tell you now that the king's army was chiefly led by his nephew, Prince Rupert, the son of his sister Elizabeth. Rupert was a fiery, brave young man, who was apt to think a battle was won before it really was, and would ride after the people he had beaten himself without waiting to see whether his help was wanted by the other captains; and so he did his uncle's cause as much harm as good.

The king's party had been the most used to war, and they prospered the most at first; but as the soldiers of the Parliament became more trained, they gained the advantage. One of the members of Parliament, a gentleman named Oliver Cromwell, soon showed himself to be a much better captain than any one else in England, and from the time he came to the chief command the Parliament always had the victory. The places of the three chief battles were Edgehill, Marston Moor, and Naseby. The first was doubtful, but the other two were great victories of the Roundheads. Just after Marston Moor, the Parliament put to death Archbishop Laud; and, at the same time, they forbade the use of the Prayer-book, and turned out all the parish priests from the churches, putting in their stead men chosen after their own fashion, and not ordained by bishops. They likewise destroyed all they disliked in the churches – the painted glass, the organs, and the carvings; and when the Puritan soldiers took possession of a town or village, they would stable their horses in the churches, use the font for a trough, and shoot at the windows as marks.

After the battle of Naseby, King Charles was in such distress that he thought he would go to the Scots, remembering that, though he had offended them by trying to make them use the Prayer-book, he had been born among them, and he thought they would prefer him to the English. But when he came, the Scottish army treated him like a prisoner, and showed him very few honors; and at last they gave him up to the English Parliament for a great sum of money.

So Charles was a prisoner to his own subjects. This Parliament is called the Long Parliament, because it sat longer than any other Parliament ever did: indeed it had passed a resolution that it could not be dissolved.

CHAPTER XXXV.

DEATH OF CHARLES I. A.D. 1649 – 1651.

The Long Parliament did not wish to have no king, only to make him do what they pleased; and then went on trying whether he would come back to reign according to their notions. He would have given up a great deal, but when they wanted him to declare that there should be no bishops in England he would never consent, for he thought there could be no real Church without bishops, as our Lord himself had appointed.

At last, after there had been much debating, and it was plain that it would never come to an end, Oliver Cromwell sent some of his officers to take King Charles into their hands, instead of the persons appointed by Parliament. So the king was prisoner to the army instead of to the parliament.

Cromwell was a very able man, and he saw that nobody could settle the difficulties about the law and the rights of the people but himself. He saw that things never would be settled while the king lived, nor by the Parliament, so he sent one of his officers, named Pryde, to turnout all the members of Parliament who would not do his will, and then the fifty who were left appointed a court of officers and lawyers to try the king. Charles was brought before them; but, as they had no right to try him, he would not say a word in answer to them. Nevertheless, they sentenced him to have his head cut off. He had borne all his troubles in the most meek and patient way, forgiving all his enemies and praying for them: and he was ready to die in the same temper. His queen was in France, and all his children were safe out of England, except his daughter Elizabeth, who was twelve years old, and little Henry, who was five. They were brought to Whitehall Palace for him to see the night before he was to die. He took the little boy on his knee, and talked a long time to Elizabeth, telling her what books to read and giving her his message to her mother and brothers; and then he told little Henry to mark what he said, and to mind that he must never be set up as a king while his elder brothers, Charles and James were alive. The little boy said through his tears, "I will be torn to pieces first." His father kissed and blessed the two children, and left them.

The next day was the 30th of January, 1649. The king was allowed to have Bishop Juxon to read and pray with him, and to give him the holy communion. After that, forgiving his enemies and praying for them, he was led to the Banqueting House at Whitehall, and out through a window, on to the scaffold hung with black cloth. He said his last prayers, and the executioner cut off his head with one blow, and held it up to the people. He was buried at night, – a light snow falling at the time, – in St. George's Chapel at Windsor, by four faithful noblemen, but they were not allowed to use any service over his grave.

The Scots were so much shocked to find what their selling of their king had come to, that they invited his eldest son, Charles, a young man of nineteen, to come and reign over them, and offered to set him on the English throne again. Young Charles came; but they were so strict that they made his life very dull and weary, since they saw sin in every amusement. However, they kept their promise of marching into England, and some of the English cavaliers joined them; but Oliver Cromwell and his army met them at

Worcester, and they were entirely beaten. Young King Charles had to go away with a few gentlemen, and he was so closely followed that they had to put him in charge of some woodmen named Penderel, who lived in Boscobel Forest. They dressed him in a rough leather suit like their own, and when the Roundhead soldiers came to search, he was hidden among the branches of an oak tree above their heads. Afterwards, a lady named Jane Lane helped him over another part of his journey, by letting him ride on horseback before her as her servant; but, when she stopped at an inn, he was very near being found out, because he did not know how to turn the spit in the kitchen when the cook asked him. However, he got safely to Brighton, which was only a little village then, and a boat took him to France, where his mother was living.

In the meantime, his young sister and brother, Elizabeth and Henry, had been sent to the Isle of Wight, to Carisbrook Castle. Elizabeth was pining away with sorrow, and before long she was found dead, with her cheek resting on her open Bible. After this, little Henry was sent to be with his mother in France.

The eldest daughter, Mary, had been married just as the war began to the Prince of Orange, who lived in Holland, and was left a widow with one little son. James, Duke of York, the second brother, had at first been in the keeping of a Parliamentary nobleman, with his brother and sister, in London; but, during a game of hide-and-seek, he crept out of the gardens and met some friends, who dressed him in girls' clothes and took him to a ship in the Thames, which carried him to Holland. Little Henrietta, the youngest, had been left, when only six weeks old, to the care of one of her mother's ladies. When she was nearly three, the lady did not think it safe to keep her any longer in England. So she stained her face and hands brown with walnut juice, to look like a gipsy, took the child upon her back, and trudged to the coast.

Little Henrietta could not speak plain, but she always called herself by a name she meant to be princess, and the lady was obliged to call her Piers, and pretend that she was a little boy, when the poor child grew angry at being treated so differently from usual, and did all she possibly could to make the strangers understand that she was no beggar boy. However, at last she was safe across the sea, and was with her mother at Paris, where the king of France, Queen Henrietta's nephew, was very kind to the poor exiles. The misfortune was, that the queen brought up little Henrietta as a Roman Catholic, and tried to make Henry one also; but he was old enough to be firm to his father's Church, and he went away to his sister in Holland. James, however did somewhat late become a Roman Catholic; and Charles would have been one, if he had cared enough about religion to do what would have lessened his chance of getting back to England as king. But these two brothers were learning no good at Paris, and were growing careless of the right and fond of pleasure. James and Henry, after a time, joined the French army, that they might learn the art of war. They were both very brave, but it was sad that when France and England went to war, they should be in the army of the enemies of their country.

CHAPTER XXXVI.

OLIVER CROMWELL. A.D. 1649 – 1660.

Oliver Cromwell felt, as has been said, that there was no one who could set matters to rights as he could in England. He had shewn that the country could not do without him, if it was to go on without the old government. Not only had he conquered and slain Charles I., and beaten that king's friends and those of his son in Scotland, but he had put down a terrible rising of the Irish, and suppressed them with much more cruelty than he generally showed.

He found that the old Long Parliament did nothing but blunder and talk, so he marched into the House one day with a company of soldiers, and sternly ordered the members all off, calling out, as he pointed to the mace that lay before the Speaker's chair, "Take away that bauble." After that he called together a fresh Parliament; but there were very few members, and those only men who would do as he bade them. The Speaker was a leather-seller named Barebones, so that this is generally known as Barebones' Parliament. By these people he was named Lord Protector of England; and as his soldiers would still do anything for him, he reigned for five years, just as a king might have done, and a good king too.

He was by no means a cruel or unmerciful man, and he did not persecute the Cavaliers more than he could help, if he was to keep up his power; though, of course, they suffered a great deal, since they had fines laid upon them, and some forfeited their estates for having resisted the Parliament. Many had to live in Holland or France, because there was no safety for them in England, and their wives went backwards and forwards to their homes to collect their rents, and obtain something to live upon. The bishops and clergy had all been driven out, and in no church was it allowable to use the Prayer-book; so there used to be secret meetings in rooms, or vaults, or in woods, where the prayers could be used as of old, and the holy sacrament administered.

For five years Cromwell was Lord Protector, but in the year 1658 he died, advising that his son Richard should be chosen Protector in his stead. Richard Cromwell was a kind, amiable gentleman, but not clever or strong like his father, and he very soon found that to govern England was quite beyond his power; so he gave up, and went to live at his own home again, while the English people gave him the nick-name Tumble-down-Dick.

No one seemed well to know what was to be done next; but General Monk, who was now at the head of the army, thought the best thing possible would be to bring back the king. A new Parliament was elected, and sent an invitation to Charles II. to come back again and reign like his forefathers. He accepted it; the fleet was sent to fetch him, and on the 29th of May, 1660, he rode into London between his brothers, James and Henry. The streets were dressed with green boughs, the windows hung with tapestry, and everyone shewed such intense joy and delight, the king said he could not think why he should have stayed away so long, since everyone was so glad to see him back again.

But the joy of his return was clouded by the deaths of his sister Mary, the Princess of Orange, and of his brother Henry, who was only just twenty. Mary left a son, William, Prince of Orange, of whom you will hear more.

The bishops were restored, and, as there had been no archbishop since Laud had been beheaded, good Juxon, who had attended King Charles at his death, was made archbishop in his room. The persons who had been put into the parishes to act as clergymen, were obliged to give place to the real original parish priest; but if he were dead, as was often the case, they were told that they might stay, if they would be ordained by the bishops and obey the Prayer-book. Some did so, some made an arrangement for keeping the parsonages, and paying a curate to take the service in church; but those who were the most really in earnest gave up everything, and were turned out – but only as they had turned out the former clergymen ten or twelve years before.

All Oliver Cromwell's army was broken up, and the men sent to their homes, except one regiment which came from Coldstream in Scotland. These would not disband, and when Charles II. heard it he said he would take them as his guards. This was the beginning of there being always a regular army of men, whose whole business it is to be soldiers, instead of any man being called from his work when he is wanted.

Charles II. promised pardon to all the rebels, but he did try and execute all who had been actually concerned in condemning his father to death.

CHAPTER XXXVII.

CHARLES II. A.D. 1660-1685.

It is sad to have to say that, after all his troubles, Charles II. disappointed everybody. Some of these disappointments could not be helped, but others were his own fault. The Puritan party thought, after they had brought him home again he should have been more favorable to them, and grumbled at the restoration of the clergymen and of the Prayer-book. The Cavaliers thought that, after all they had gone through for him and his father, he ought to have rewarded them more; but he said truly enough, that if he had made a nobleman of everyone who had deserved well of him, no place but Salisbury Plain would have been big enough for the House of Lords to meet upon. Then those gentlemen who had got into debt to raise soldiers for the king's service, and had paid fines, or had to sell their estates, felt it hard not to have them again; but when a Roundhead gentleman had honestly bought the property, it would have been still more unjust to turn them out. These two old names of Cavaliers and Roundheads began to turn into two others even more absurd. The Cavalier set came to be called Tories, an Irish name for a robber, and the Puritans got the Scotch name of Whigs, which means buttermilk.

It would have taken a very strong, wise, and good man to deal rightly with two such different sets of people; but though Charles II. was a very clever man, he was neither wise nor good. He could not bear to vex himself, nor anybody else; and, rather than be teased, would grant almost anything that was asked of him. He was so bright and lively, and made such droll, good-natured answers, that everyone liked him who came near him; but he had no steady principle, only to stand easy with everybody, and keep as much power for himself as he could without giving offence. He loved pleasure much better than duty, and kept about him a set of people who amused him, but were a disgrace to his court. They even took money from the French king to persuade Charles against helping the Dutch in their war against the French. The Dutch went to war with the English upon this, and there were many terrible sea- fights, in which James, Duke of York, the king's brother, shewed himself a good and brave sailor.

The year 1665 is remembered as that in which there was a dreadful sickness in London, called the plague. People died of it often after a very short illness, and it was so infectious that it was difficult to escape it. When a person in a house was found to have it, the door was fastened up and marked with a red cross in chalk, and no one was allowed to go out or in; food was set down outside to be fetched in, and carts came round to take away the dead, who were all buried together in long ditches. The plague was worst in the summer and autumn; as winter came on more recovered and fewer sickened, and at last this frightful sickness was ended; and by God's good mercy, it has never since that year come to London.

The next year 1666, there was a fire in London, which burnt down whole streets, with their churches, and even destroyed St. Paul's Cathedral. Perhaps it did good by burning down the dirty old houses and narrow streets where the plague might have lingered, but it was a fearsome misfortune. It was only stopped at last by blowing up a space with gunpowder all round it, so that the flames might have no way to pass on. The king and his brother came and were very helpful in giving orders about this, and in finding shelter for many poor, homeless people.

There was a good deal of disturbance in Scotland when the king wanted to bring back the bishops and the Prayer-book. Many of the Scots would not go to church, and met on hills and moors to have their prayers in their own way. Soldiers were sent to disperse them, and there was much fierce, bitter feeling. Archbishop Sharpe was dragged out of his carriage and killed, and then there was a civil war, in which the king's men prevailed; but the Whigs were harshly treated, and there was great discontent.

The country was much troubled because the king and queen had no children: and the Duke of York was a Roman Catholic. A strange story was got up that there was what was called a popish plot for killing the king, and putting James on the throne. Charles himself laughed at it, for he knew everyone liked him and disliked his brother: "No one would kill me to make you king, James," he said; but in his easy, selfish way, when he found that all the country believed in it, and wanted to have the men they fancied guilty put to death, he did not try to save their lives.

Soon after this false plot, there was a real one called the Rye-house Plot. Long ago, the king had pretended to marry a girl named Lucy Waters and they had a son whom he had made Duke of Monmouth, but who could not reign because there had been no right marriage. However, Lord Russell and some other gentlemen, who ought to have know better, so hated the idea of the Duke of York being king, that they joined in the Ryehouse Plot for killing the duke, and forcing the king to make Monmouth his heir. Some of the more unprincipled sort, who had joined them, even meant to shoot Charles and James together on the way to the Newmarket races. However, the plot was found out, and the leaders were put to death. Lord Russell's wife, Lady Rachel, sat by him all the time of his trial, and was his great comfort to the last. Monmouth was pardoned, but fled away into Holland.

The best thing to be said of Charles II. was that he made good men bishops, and he never was angry when they spoke out boldly about his wicked ways; but then, he never tried to leave them off, and he spent the very last Sunday of his life among his bad companions, playing at cards and listening to idle songs. Just after this came a stroke of apoplexy, and, while he lay dying on his bed, he sent for a Roman Catholic priest, and was received into the Church of Rome, in which he had really believed most of his life – though he had never dared to own it, for fear of losing his crown. So, as he was living a lie, of course the fruits showed themselves in his selfish, wasted life.

It was in this reign that two grand books were written. John Milton, a blind scholar and poet, who, before he lost his sight, had been Oliver Cromwell's secretary, wrote his Paradise Lost, or rather dictated it to his daughters; and John Bunyan, a tinker, who had been a Puritan preacher, wrote the Pilgrim's Progress.

CHAPTER XXXVIII.

JAMES II. A.D. 1685 – 1688.

James II. had, at least, been honest in openly joining the Church in which he believed; but the people disliked and distrusted him, and he had not the graces of his brother to gain their hearts with, but was grave, sad, and stern.

The Duke of Monmouth came across from Holland, and was proclaimed king in his uncle's stead at Exeter. Many people in the West of England joined him, and at Taunton, in Somersetshire, he was received by rows of little girls standing by the gate in white frocks, strewing flowers before him. But at Sedgemoor he was met by the army, and his friends were routed; he himself fled away, and at last was caught hiding in a ditch, dressed in a laborer's smock frock, and with his pockets full of peas from the fields. He was taken to London, tried, and executed. He did not deserve much pity, but James ought not to have let the people who favored him be cruelly treated. Sir George Jeffreys, the chief justice, was sent to try all who had been concerned, from Winchester to Exeter; and he hung so many, and treated all so savagely, that his progress was called the Bloody Assize. Even the poor little maids at Taunton were thrown into a horrible, dirty jail, and only released on their parents paying a heavy sum of money for them.

This was a bad beginning for James's reign; and the English grew more angry and suspicious when they saw that he favored Roman Catholics more than anyone else, and even put them into places that only clergymen of the Church of England could fill. Then he put forth a decree, declaring that a person might be chosen to any office in the State, whether he were a member of the English Church or no; and he commanded that every clergyman should read it from his pulpit on Sunday mornings. Archbishop Sancroft did not think it a right thing for clergymen to read, and he and six more bishops presented a petition to the king against being obliged to read it. One of these was Thomas Ken, Bishop of Bath and Wells, who wrote the morning hymn, "Awake, my soul, and with the sun," and the evening hymn, "All praise to Thee, my God, this night." Instead of listening to their petition, the king had all the seven bishops sent to the Tower, and tried for libel – that is, for malicious writing. All England was full of anxiety, and when at last the jury gave the verdict of "not guilty," the whole of London rang with shouts of joy, and the soldiers in their camp shouted still louder.

This might have been a warning to the king; for he thought that, as he paid the army, they were all on his side, and would make the people bear whatever he pleased. The chief comfort people had was in thinking their troubles would only last during his reign: for his first wife, an Englishwoman, had only left him two daughters, Mary and Anne, and Mary was married to her cousin William, Prince of Orange, who was a great enemy of the King of France and of the pope; and Anne's husband, Prince George, brother to the King of Denmark, was a Protestant. He was a dull man, and people laughed at him – because, whenever he heard any news, he never said anything but *"Est il possible?"* is it possible? But he had a little son, of whom there was much hope.

But James had married again, Mary Beatrice d'Este, an Italian princess; and, though none of her babies had lived before, at last she had a little son who was healthy and likely to live, and who was christened James. Poor little boy! Everyone was so angry and disappointed that he should have come into the world at all, that a story was put about that he was not the son of the king and queen, but a strange baby who had been carried into the queen's room in a warming-pan, because James was resolved to prevent Mary and William from reigning.

Only silly people could believe such a story as this; but all the Whigs, and most of the Tories, thought in earnest that it was a sad thing for the country to have an heir to the throne brought up by a Roman Catholic, and to think it right to treat his subjects as James was treating them. Some would have been patient, and have believed that God would bring it right, but others were resolved to put a stop to the evils they expected; and, knowing what was the state of people's minds, William of Orange set forth from Holland, and landed at Torbay. Crowds of people came to meet him, and to call on him. It was only three years since the Bloody Assize, and they had not forgotten it in those parts. King James heard that one person after another had gone to the Prince of Orange, and he thought it not safe for his wife and child to be any longer in England. So, quietly, one night he put them in charge of a French nobleman who had been visiting him, and who took them to the Thames, where, after waiting in the dark under a church wall, he brought them a boat, and they reached a ship which took them safely to France.

King James staid a little longer. He did not mind when he heard that Prince George of Denmark had gone to the Prince of Orange, but only laughed, and said "*Est il possible?*" but when he heard his daughter Anne, to whom he had always been kind, was gone too, the tears came into his eyes, and he said, "God help me, my own children are deserting me." He would have put himself at the head of the army, but he found that if he did so he was likely to be made prisoner and carried to William. So he disguised himself and set off for France; but at Faversham, some people who took him for a Roman Catholic priest seized him, and he was sent back to London. However, as there was nothing the Prince of Orange wished so little as to keep him in captivity, he was allowed to escape again, and this time he safely reached France, where he was very kindly welcomed, and had the palace of St. Germain given him for a dwelling-place.

It was on the 4th of November, 1688, that William landed, and the change that now took place is commonly called the English Revolution.

We must think of the gentlemen, during these reigns, as going about in very fine laced and ruffled coats, and the most enormous wigs. You know the Roundheads had short hair and the Cavaliers long: so people were ashamed to have short hair, and wore wigs to hide it if it would not grow, till everybody came to have shaven heads, and monstrous wigs in great curls on their shoulders: and even little boys' hair was made to look as like a wig as possible. The barber had the wig every morning to fresh curl, and make it white with hair powder, so that everyone might look like an old man, with a huge quantity of white hair.

CHAPTER XXXIX.

WILLIAM III. AND MARY II. 1689 – 1702.

When James II. proved to be entirely gone, the Parliament agreed to offer the crown to William of Orange – the next heir after James's children – and Mary, his wife, James's eldest daughter; but not until there had been new conditions made, which would prevent the kings from ever being so powerful again as they had been since the time of Henry VII. Remember, Magna Carta, under King John, gave the power to the nobles. They lost it by the wars of the Roses, and the Tudor kings gained it; but the Stuart kings could not keep it, and the House of Commons became the strongest power in the kingdom, by the Revolution of 1688.

The House of Commons is made up of persons chosen – whenever there is a general election – by the men who have a certain amount of property in each county and large town. There must be a fresh election, or choosing again every seven years; also, whenever the sovereign dies; and the sovereign can dissolve the Parliament – that is, break it up – and have a fresh election whenever it is thought right. But above the House of Commons stands the House of Lords, or Peers. These are not chosen, but the eldest son, or next heir of each lord, succeeds to his seat upon his death; and fresh peerages are given as rewards to great generals, great lawyers, or people who have deserved well of their country. When a law has to be made, it has first to be agreed to by a majority – that is, the larger number – of the Commons, then by a majority of the Lords, and lastly, by the king or queen. The sovereign's council are called the ministers, and if the

Houses of Parliament do not approve of their way of carrying on the government they vote against their proposals, and this generally makes them resign, that others may be chosen in their place who may please the country better.

This arrangement has gone on ever since William and Mary came in. However, James II. still had many friends, only they had been out of reach at the first alarm. The Latin word for James is Jacobus, and, therefore, they were called Jacobites. All Roman Catholics were, of course, Jacobites; and there were other persons who, though grieved at the king's conduct, did not think it right to rise against him and drive him away; and, having taken an oath to obey him, held that it would be wrong to swear obedience to anyone else while he was alive. Archbishop Sancroft was one of these. He thought it wrong in the new queen, Mary, to consent to take her father's place; and when she sent to ask his blessing, he told her to ask her father's first, as, without that, his own would do her little good. Neither he nor Bishop Ken, nor some other bishops, nor a good many more of the clergy, would take the oaths to William, or put his name instead of that of James in the prayers at church. They rather chose to be turned out of their bishoprics and parishes, and to live in poverty. They were called the non-jurors, or not-swearers.

Louis, King of France, tried to send James back, and gave him the service of his fleet; but it was beaten by Admiral Russell, off Cape La Hogue. Poor James could not help crying out, "See my brave English sailors!" One of Charles's old officers, Lord Dundee, raised an army of Scots in James's favor, but he was killed just as he had won the battle of Killicrankie; and there was no one to take up the cause just then, and the Scotch Whigs were glad of the change.

Most of James's friends, the Roman Catholics, were in Ireland, and Louis lent him an army with which to go thither and try to win his crown back. He got on pretty well in the South, but in the North – where Oliver Cromwell had given lands to many of his old soldiers – he met with much more resistance. At Londonderry, the apprentice boys shut the gates of the town and barred them against him. A clergyman named George Walker took the command of the city, and held it out for a hundred and five days against him, till everyone was nearly starved to death – and at last help came from England. William himself came to Ireland, and the father and son-in-law met in battle on the banks of the Boyne, on the 1st of July, 1690. James was routed; and large numbers of the Irish Protestants have ever since kept the 1st of July as a great holiday – commemorating the victory by wearing orange lilies and orange-colored scarfs.

James was soon obliged to leave Ireland, and his friends there were severely punished. In the meantime, William was fighting the French in Holland – as he had done nearly all his life – while Mary governed the kingdom at home. She was a handsome, stately lady, and was much respected; and there was great grief when she died of the small-pox, never having had any children. It was settled upon this that William should go on reigning as long as he lived, and then that Princess Anne should be queen; and if she left no children, that the next after her should be the youngest daughter of Elizabeth, daughter of James I. Her name was Sophia, and she was married to Ernest of Brunswick, Elector of Hanover. It was also settled that no Roman Catholic, nor even anyone who married a Roman Catholic, could ever be on the English throne.

Most of the Tories disliked this Act of Settlement; and nobody had much love for King William, who was a thin, spare man, with a large, hooked nose, and very rough, sharp manners – perhaps the more sharp because he was never in good health, and suffered terribly from the asthma. However, he managed to keep all the countries under him in good order, and he was very active, and always at war with the French. Towards the end of his reign a fresh quarrel began, in which all Europe took part. The King of Spain died without children, and the question was who should reign after him. The King of France had married one sister of this king, and the Emperor of Germany was the son of her aunt. One wanted to make his grandson king of Spain, the other his son, and so there was a great war. William III. took part against the French – as he had always been their enemy; but just as the war was going to begin, as he was riding near his palace of Hampton Court, his horse trod into a mole-hill, and he fell, breaking his collar bone; and this hurt his weak chest so much that he died in a few days, in the year 1702. The Jacobites were very glad to be rid of him, and used to drink the health of the "little gentleman in a black velvet coat," meaning the mole which had caused his death.

CHAPTER XL.

ANNE. A.D. 1702 – 1714.

Queen Anne, the second daughter of James II., began to reign on the death of William III. She was a well-meaning woman, but very weak and silly; and any person who knew how to manage her could make her have no will of her own. The person who had always had such power over her has Sarah Jennings, a lady in her train, who had married an officer named John Churchill. As this gentleman had risen in the army, he proved to be one of the most able generals who ever lived. He was made a peer, and, step by step, came to be Duke of Marlborough. It was he and his wife who, being Whigs, had persuaded Anne to desert her father; and, now she was queen, she did just as they pleased. The duchess was mistress of the robes, and more queen at home than Anne was; and the duke commanded the army which was sent to fight against the French, to decide who should be king of Spain. An expedition was sent to Spain, which gained the rock of Gibraltar, and this has been kept by the English ever since.

Never were there greater victories than were gained by the English and German forces together, under the Duke of Marlborough and Prince Eugene of Savoy, who commanded the Emperor's armies. The first and greatest battle of them all was fought at Blenheim, in Bavaria, when the French were totally defeated, with great loss. Marlborough was rewarded by the queen and nation buying an estate for him, which was called Blenheim, where woods were planted so as to imitate the position of his army before the battle, and a grand house built and filled with pictures recording his adventures. The other battles were all in the Low Countries – at Ramillies, Oudenard, and Malplaquet. The city of Lisle was taken after a long siege, and not a summer went by without tidings coming of some great victory, and the queen going in a state coach to St. Paul's Cathedral to return thanks for it.

But all this glory of her husband made the Duchess of Marlborough more proud and overbearing. She thought the queen could not do without her, and so she left off taking any trouble to please her; nay, she would sometimes scold her more rudely than any real lady would do to any woman, however much below her in rank. Sometimes she brought the poor queen to tears; and on the day on which Anne went in state to St. Paul's, to return thanks for the victory of Oudenarde, she was seen to be crying all the way from St. James's Palace in her coach, with the six cream-colored horses, because the duchess had been scolding her for putting on her jewels in the way she liked best, instead of in the duchess's way.

Now, Duchess Sarah had brought to the palace, to help to wait on the queen, a poor cousin of her own, named Abigail Masham, a much more smooth and gentle person, but rather deceitful. When the mistress of the robes was unkind and insolent, the queen used to complain to Mrs. Masham; and by-and-by Abigail told her how to get free. There was a gentleman, well known to Mrs. Masham – Mr. Harley, a member of Parliament and a Tory, and she brought him in by the back stairs to see the queen, without the duchess knowing it. He undertook, if the queen would stand by him, to be her minister, and to turn out the Churchills and their Whig friends, send away the tyrant duchess, and make peace, so that the duke might not be wanted any more. In fact, the war had gone on quite long enough; the power of the King of France was broken, and he was an old man, whom it was cruel to press further; but this was not what Anne cared about so much as getting free of the duchess. There was great anger and indignation among all the Whigs at the breaking off of the war in the midst of so much glory; and, besides, the nation did not keep its engagements to the others with whom it had allied itself. Marlborough himself was not treated as a man deserved who had won so much honor for his country, and he did not keep his health many years after his fall. Once, when he felt his mind getting weak, he looked up at his own picture at Blenheim, taken when he was one of the handsomest, most able, and active men in Europe, and said sadly, "Ah! that *was* a man."

Mr. Harley was made Earl of Oxford, and managed the queen's affairs for her. He and the Tories did not at all like the notion of the German family of Brunswick – Sophia and her son George – who were to reign next, and they allowed the queen to look towards her own family a little more. Her father had died in exile, but there remained the young brother whom she had disowned, and whom the French and the Jacobites called King James III. If he would have joined the English Church Anne would have gladly invited him, and many of the English would have owned him as the right king; but he was too honest to give up his faith, and the queen could do nothing for him.

Till her time the Scots – though since James I. they had been under the same king as England – had had a separate Parliament, Lords and Commons, who sat at Edinburgh; but in the reign of Queen Anne the Scottish Parliament was united to the English one, and the members of it had to come to Westminster. This made many Scotsmen so angry that they became Jacobites; but as every body knew that the queen was a gentle, well-meaning old lady, nobody wished to disturb her, and all was quiet as long as she lived, so that her reign was an unusually tranquil one at home, though there were such splendid victories abroad. It was a time, too, when there were almost as many able writers as in Queen Elizabeth's time. The two books written at that day, which you are most likely to have heard of, are Robinson Crusoe, written by Daniel Defoe, and Alexander Pope's translation of Homer's Iliad.

Anne's Tory friends did not make her happy; they used to quarrel among themselves and frightened her; and after one of their disputes she had an attack of apoplexy, and soon died of it, in the year 1714.

It was during Anne's reign that it became the fashion to drink tea and coffee. One was brought from China, and the other from Arabia, not very long before, and they were very dear indeed. The ladies used to drink tea out of little cups of egg-shell china, and the clever gentlemen, who were called the wits, used to meet and talk at coffeehouses, and read newspapers, and discuss plays and poems; also, the first magazine was then begun. It was called "The Spectator," and was managed by Mr. Addison. It came out once a week, and laughed at or blamed many of the foolish and mischievous habits of the time. Indeed it did much to draw people out of the bad ways that had come in with Charles II.

CHAPTER XLI.

GEORGE I. A.D. 1714 – 1725.

The Electress Sophia, who had always desired to be queen of England, had died a few months before Queen Anne; and her son George, who liked his own German home much better than the trouble of reigning in a strange country, was in no hurry to come, and waited to see whether the English would not prefer the young James Stuart. But as no James arrived George set off, rather unwillingly, and was received in London in a dull kind of way. He hardly knew any English, and was obliged sometimes to talk bad Latin and sometimes French, when he consulted with his ministers. He did not bring a queen with him, for he had quarrelled with his wife, and shut her up in a castle in Germany; but he had a son, also named George, who had a very clever, handsome wife – Caroline of Anspach, a German princess; but the king was jealous of them, and generally made them live abroad.

Just when it was too late, and George I. had thoroughly settled into his kingdom, the Jacobites in the North of England and in Scotland began to make a stir, and invited James Stuart over to try to gain the kingdom. The Jacobites used to call him James III., but the Whigs called him the Pretender; and the Tories used, by way of a middle course, to call him the Chevalier – the French word for a knight, as that he certainly was, whether he were king or pretender. A white rose was the Jacobite mark, and the Whigs still held to the orange lily and orange ribbon, for the sake of William of Orange.

The Jacobite rising did not come to any good. Two battles were fought between the king's troops and the Jacobites – one in England and the other in Scotland – on the very same day. The Scottish one was at Sheriff-muir, and was so doubtful, that the old Scottish song about it ran thus –

> Some say that we won,
> And some say the they won,
> Some say that none won
> At a', man;
>
> But of one thing I'm sure,
> That at Sheriff-muir
> A battle there was,
> Which I saw, man.
>
> And we ran, and they ran,
> And they ran, and we ran,
> And we ran, and they ran –
> Awa, man.

The English one was at Preston, and in it the Jacobites were all defeated and made prisoners; so that when their friend the Chevalier landed in Scotland, he found that nothing could be done, and had to go back again to Italy, where he generally lived, under the Pope's protection; and where he married a Polish princess and had two sons, whom he named Charles Edward and Henry.

This rising of the Jacobites took place in the year 1715, and is, therefore, generally called the Rebellion of the Fifteen. The chief noblemen who were engaged in it were taken to London to be tried. Three were beheaded; one was saved upon his wife's petition; and one, the Earl of Nithsdale, by the cleverness of his wife. She was allowed to go and see him in the Tower, and she took a tall lady in with her, who contrived to wear a double set of outer garments. The friend went away, after a time; and then, after waiting till the guard was changed, Lady Nithsdale dressed her husband in the clothes that had been brought in: and he, too, went away, with the hood over his face and a handkerchief up to his eyes, so that the guard might take him for the other lady, crying bitterly at parting with the earl. The wife, meantime, remained for some time, talking and walking up and down as heavily as she could, till the time came when she would naturally be obliged to leave him – when, as she passed by his servant, she said to him that "My lord will not be ready for the candles just yet," – and then left the Tower, and went to a little lodging in a back street, where she found her husband, and where they both lay hid while the search for Lord Nithsdale was going on, and where they heard the knell tolling when his friends, the other lords, were being led out to have their heads cut off. Afterwards, they made their escape to France, where most of the Jacobites who had been concerned in the rising were living, as best they could, on small means – and some of them by becoming soldiers of the King of France.

England was prosperous in the time of George I., and the possessions of the country in India were growing, from a merchant's factory here and there, to large lands and towns. But the English never liked King George, nor did he like them; and he generally spent his time in his own native country of Hanover. He was taking a drive there in his coach, when a letter was thrown in at the window. As he was reading it, a sudden stroke of apoplexy came on, and he died in a few hours' time. No one ever knew what was in the letter, but some thought it was a letter reproaching him with his cruelty to his poor wife, who had died in her prison about eight months before. He died in the year 1725.

Gentlemen were leaving off full-bottomed wigs now, and wearing smaller ones; and younger men had their own hair powdered, and tied up with ribbon in a long tail behind, called a queue. Ladies powdered their hair, and raised it to an immense height, and also wore monstrous hoops, long ruffles, and high-heeled shoes. Another odd fashion was that ladies put black patches on their faces, thinking they made them handsomer. Both ladies and gentlemen took snuff, and carried beautiful snuff-boxes.

CHAPTER XLII.

GEORGE II. A.D. 1725 – 1760.

The reign of George II. was a very warlike one. Indeed he was the last king of England who ever was personally in a battle; and, curiously enough, this battle – that of Fontenoy – was the last that a king of France also was present in. It was, however, not a very interesting battle; and it was not clear who really won it, nor are wars of this time very easy to understand.

The battle of Fontenoy was fought in the course of a great war to decide who would be emperor of Germany, in which France and England took different sides; and this made Charles Edward Stuart, the eldest son of James, think it was a good moment for trying once again to get back the crown of his forefathers. He was a fine-looking young man, with winning manners, and a great deal more spirit than his father: and when he landed in Scotland with a very few followers, one Highland gentleman after another was so delighted with him that they all brought their clans to join him, and he was at the head of quite a large force, with which he took possession of the town of Edinburgh; but he never could take the castle. The English army was most of it away fighting in Germany, and the soldiers who met him at Prestonpans, close to Edinburgh, were not well managed, and were easily beaten by the Highlanders. Then he marched straight on into England: and there was great terror, for the Highlanders – with their plaids, long swords, and strange language – were thought to be all savage robbers, and the Londoners expected to have every house and shop ruined and themselves murdered:

though on the whole the Highlanders behaved very well. They would probably have really entered London if they had gone on, and reached it before the army could come home, but they grew discontented and frightened at being so far away from their own hills; and at Derby. Charles Edward was obliged to let them turn back to Scotland.

The English army had come back by this time, and the Scots were followed closely, getting more sad and forlorn, and losing men in every day's march, till at last, after they had reached Scotland again, they made a stand against the English under the king's second son, William, Duke of Cumberland, at the heath of Culloden. There they were entirely routed, and the prince had to fly, and hide himself in strange places and disguises, much as his great uncle, Charles II., had done before him. A young lady named Flora Macdonald took him from one of the Western Isles to another in a boat as her Irish maid, Betty Bourke; and, at another time, he was his in a sort of bower, called the cage, woven of branches of trees on a hill side, where he lived with three Highlanders, who used to go out by turns to get food. One of them once brought him a piece of ginger-bread as a treat – for they loved him heartily for being patient, cheerful, and thankful for all they did for him; and when at last he found a way of reaching France, and shook hands with them on bidding the farewell, one of them tied up his right hand, and vowed that no meaner person should ever touch it.

The Empress Maria Theresa, of Germany, had a long war with Frederick, King of Prussia, who was nephew to George II., and a very clever and brave man, who made his little kingdom of Prussia very warlike and brave. But he was not a very good man, and these were sad times among the great people, for few of them thought much about being good: and there were clever Frenchmen who laughed at all religion. You know one of the Psalms, "The fool hath said in his heart, there is no God." There were a great many such fools at that time, and their ways, together with the selfishness of the nobles, soon brought terrible times to France, and all the countries round.

The wars under George II. were by sea as well as by land: and, likewise, in the distant countries where Englishmen, on the one hand, and Frenchmen, on the other, had made those new homes that we call colonies. In North America, both English and French had large settlements; and when the kings at home were at war, there were likewise battles in these distant parts, and the Indians were stirred up to take part with the one side or the other. They used to attack the homes of the settlers, burn them, kill and torment the men, and keep the children to bring up among their own. The English had, in general, the advantage, especially in Canada, where the brave young General Wolfe led an attack, on the very early morning, to the Heights of Abraham, close to the town of Quebec. He was struck down by a shot early in the fight, and lay on the ground with a few officers round him. "They run, they run!" he heard them cry. "Who run?" he asked. "The French run." "Then I die happy," he said; and it was by this battle that England won Lower Canada, with many French inhabitants, whose descendants still speak their old language.

In the East Indies, too, there was much fighting. The English and French both had merchants there; and these had native soldiers to guard them, and made friends with the native princes. When these princes quarreled they helped them, and so obtained a larger footing. But in this reign the English power was nearly ended in a very sad way. An Indian army came suddenly down on Calcutta. Many English got on board the ships, but those who could not – 146 in number – were shut up all night in a small room, in the hottest time of the year, and they were so crushed together and suffocated by the heat that, when the morning came, there were only twenty-three of them alive. This dreadful place was known as the Black Hole of Calcutta. The next year Calcutta was won back again; and the English, under Colonel Clive, gained so much ground that the French had no power left in India, and the English could go on obtaining more and more land, riches and power.

George II. had lost his eldest son, Frederick, Prince of Wales, and his lively and clever wife, Queen Caroline, many years before his death. His chief ministers were, first, Sir Robert Walpole, and afterwards the Earl of Chatham – able men, who knew how to manage the country through all these wars. The king died at last, quite suddenly when sixty-eight years old, in the year 1760.

CHAPTER XLIII.

GEORGE III. A.D. 1760 – 1785.

After George II. reigned his grandson, George III., the son of Frederick, Prince of Wales, who had died before his father. The Princess of Wales was a good woman, who tried to bring up her children well; and George III. was a dutiful son to her, and a good, faithful man – always caring more to do right than for anything else. He had been born in England, and did not feel as if Hanover were his home, as his father and grandfather had done, but loved England, and English people, and ways. When he was at Windsor, he used to ride or walk about like a country squire, and he had a ruddy, hearty face and manner, that made him sometimes be called Farmer George; and he had an odd way of saying "What? what?" when he was spoken to, which made him be laughed at; but he was as good and true as any man who ever lived: and when he thought a thing was right, he was as firm as a rock in holding to it. He married a German princess named Charlotte, and they did their utmost to make all those about them good. They had a very large family – no less than fourteen children – and some old people still remember what a beautiful sight it was when, after church on Sunday, the king and queen and their children used to walk up and down the stately terrace at Windsor Castle, with a band playing, and everyone who was respectably dressed allowed to come in and look at them.

Just after George III. came to the crown, a great war broke out in the English colonies in America. A new tax had been made. A tax means the money that has to be given to the Government of a country to pay the judges and their officers, the soldiers and sailors, to keep up ships and buy weapons, and do all that is wanted to protect us and keep us in order. Taxes are sometimes made by calling on everybody to pay money in proportion to what they have – say threepence for every hundred pounds; sometimes they are made by putting what is called a duty on something that is bought and sold – making it sell for more than its natural price – so that the Government gets the money above the right cost. This is generally done with things that people could live without, and had better not buy too much of – such as spirits, tobacco, and hair powder. And as tea was still a new thing in England, which only fine ladies drank, it was thought useless, and there was a heavy duty laid upon it when the king wanted money. Now, the Americans got their tea straight from China, and thought it was unfair that they should pay tax on it. So, though they used it much more than the English then did, they gave it up, threw whole ship-loads of it into the harbor at Boston, and resisted the soldiers. A gentleman named George Washington took the command, and they declared they would fight for freedom from the mother country. The French were beginning to think freedom was a fine thing, and at first a few French gentlemen came over to fight among the Americans, and then the king Louis XVI., quarreled with George III., and helped them openly.

There was a very clever man among the Americans named Benjamin Franklin, a printer by trade, but who made very curious discoveries. One of them was that lightning comes from the strange power men call electricity, and that there are some substances which it will run along, so that it came be brought down to the ground without doing any mischief – especially metallic wires. He made sure of it by flying a kite, with such an iron wire up to the clouds when there was a thunder- storm. The lightning was attracted by the wire, ran down the wet string of the kite, and only glanced off when it came to a silk ribbon – because electricity will not go along silk. After this, such wires were fastened to buildings, and carried down into the ground, to convey away the force of the lightning. Perhaps you have seen them on the tops of churches or tall buildings; they are called conductors. Franklin was a plain-spoken, homely dressing man; and when he was sent to Paris on the affairs of the Americans, all the great ladies and gentlemen went into raptures about his beautiful simplicity, and began to imitate him, in a very affected, ridiculous way.

In the meantime, the war went on between America and England, year after year; and the Americans became trained soldiers and got the better, so that George III. was advised to give up his rights over them. Old Lord Chatham, his grandfather's minister, who had long been too sick and feeble to undertake any public business, thought it so bad for the country to give anything up, that he came down to the House of Lords to make a speech against doing so; but he was not strong enough for the exertion, and had only just done speaking when he fainted away, and his son, William Pitt, was called out of the House of Commons to help carry him away to his coach. He was taken home, and died in a few day's time.

The war went on, but when it had lasted seven years, the English felt that peace must be made; and so George III. gave up his rights to all that country that is called the United States of America. The United States set up a Government of their own, which has gone on ever since, without a king, but with a President who is freshly chosen every four years, and for whom every citizen has a vote.

As if to make up for what was lost in the West, the English were winning a great deal in the East Indies, chiefly from a great prince called Tipoo Sahib, who was very powerful, and at one time took a number of English officers prisoners and drove them to his city of Seringapatam, chained together in pairs, and kept them half starved in a prison, where several died; but he was defeated and killed. They were set free by their countrymen, after nearly two years of grievous hardship.

CHAPTER XLIV.

GEORGE III. A.D. 1785 – 1810.

The chief sorrow of George III. was that his eldest sons were wild, disobedient young men. George, Prince of Wales, especially, was very handsome, and extremely proud of his own beauty. He was called the First Gentleman in Europe, and set the fashion in every matter of taste; but he spent and wasted money to a shameful amount, and was full of bad habits; besides which, he used to set himself in every way in his power to vex and contradict his father and mother, whom he despised for their plain simple ways and their love of duty. The next two brothers – Frederick, Duke of York, and William, Duke of Clarence – had also very bad habits; but they went astray from carelessness, and did not wilfully oppose their father, like their eldest brother.

William Pitt, son of Lord Chatham, was Prime Minister. He thought that the Roman Catholics in England ought to have the same rights as the king's other subjects, and not be hindered from being members of Parliament, judges, or, indeed, from holding any office, and he wanted to bring a bill into Parliament for this purpose. But the king thought that for him to consent would be contrary to the oath he had sworn when he was crowned, and which had been drawn up when William of Orange came over. Nothing would make George III. break his word, and he remained firm, though he was so harassed and distressed that he fell ill, and lost the use of his reason for a time. There were questions whether the regency – that is, the right to act as king – should be given to the son, who, though his heir, was so unlike him, when he recovered; and there was a great day of joy throughout the nation, when he went in state to St. Paul's Cathedral to return thanks.

In the meantime, terrible troubles were going on in France. Neither the kings nor nobles had, for ages past, any notion of their proper duties to people under them, but had ground them down so hard that at last they could bear it no longer; and there was a great rising up throughout the country, which is known as the French Revolution. The king who was then reigning was a good and kind man, Louis XVI., who would gladly have put things in better order; but he was not as wise or firm as he was good, and the people hated him for the evil doings of his forefathers. So, while he was trying to make up his mind what to do, the power was taken out of his hands, and he, with his wife, sister, and two children, were shut up in prison. An evil spirit came into the people, and made them believe that the only way to keep themselves free would be to get rid of all who had been great people in the former days. So they set up a machine for cutting off heads, called the guillotine, and there, day after day, nobles and priests, gentlemen and ladies – even the king, queen, and princess, were brought and slain. The two children were not guillotined, but the poor little boy, only nine years old, was worse off than if he had been, for the cruel wretches who kept him called him the wolf-cub, and said he was to be got rid of, and they kept him alone in a dark, dirty room, and used him so ill that he pined to death. Many French gentry and clergymen fled to England, and there were kindly treated and helped to live; and the king's brother, now the rightful king himself, found a home there too.

At last the French grew weary of this horrible bloodshed; but, as they could not manage themselves, a soldier named Napoleon Bonaparte, by his great cleverness and the victories he gained over other nations, succeeded in getting all the power. His victories were wonderful. He beat the Germans, the Italians, the Russians, and conquered wherever he went. There was only one nation he never could beat, and that was the English; though he very much wanted to have come over here with a great fleet and army, and have conquered our island. All over England people got ready. All the men learnt something of how to be soldiers, and made themselves into regiments of volunteers; and careful watch was kept against the quantities of flat-bottomed boats that Bonaparte had made ready to bring his troops across the English Channel. But no one had ships and sailors like the English; and, besides, they had the greatest sea-captain who ever lived, whose name was Horatio Nelson. When the French went under Napoleon to try to conquer Egypt and all the East, Nelson went after them with his ships, and beat the whole French fleet, though it was a great deal larger than his own, at the mouth of the Nile, blowing up the Admiral's ship, and taking or burning many more. Afterward, when the King of Denmark was being made to take part against England, Nelson's fleet sailed to Copenhagen, fought a sharp battle, and took all the Danish ships. And lastly, when Spain had made friends with France, and both their fleets had joined together against England, Lord Nelson fought them both off Cape Trafalgar, and gained the greatest of all his victories; but it was his last, for a Frenchman on the mast-head shot him through the backbone, and he died the same night. No one should ever forget the order he gave to all his sailors in all the ships before the battle – "England expects every man to do his duty."

After the battle of Trafalgar the sea was cleared of the enemy's ships, and there was no more talk of invading England. Indeed, though Bonaparte overran nearly all the Continent of Europe, the smallest strip of sea was enough to stop him, for his ships could not stand before the English ones.

All this time English affairs were managed by Mr. Pitt, Lord Chatham's son; but he died the very same year as Lord Nelson was killed, 1805, and then his great rival, Mr. Fox, was minister in his stead: but he, too, died very soon, and affairs were managed by less clever men, but who were able to go on in the line that Pitt had marked out for them: and that was, of standing up with all their might against Bonaparte – though he now called himself the Emperor, Napoleon I., and was treading down every country in Europe.

The war time was a hard one at home in England, for everything was very dear and the taxes were high; but everyone felt that the only way to keep the French away was to go on fighting with them, and trying to help the people in the countries they seized upon. So the whole country stood up bravely against them.

Sad trouble came on the good old king in his later years. He lost his sight, and, about the same time, died his youngest child, the Princess Amelia, of whom he was very fond. His grief clouded his mind again, and there was no recovery this time. He was shut up in some rooms at Windsor Castle, where he had music to amuse him, and his good wife, Queen Charlotte, watched over him carefully as long as she lived.

CHAPTER XLV.

GEORGE III. – THE REGENCY. A.D. 1810 – 1820.

When George III. lost his senses, the government was given to his son, the Prince of Wales – the Prince Regent as he was called. Regent means a person ruling instead of the king. Everyone expected that, as he had always quarreled with his father, he would change everything and have different ministers; but instead of that, he went on just as had been done before, fighting with the French, and helping every country that tried to lift up its head against Bonaparte.

Spain was one of these countries. Napoleon had managed to get the king, and queen, and eldest son, all into his hands together, shut them up as prisoners in France, and made his own brother king. But the Spaniards were too brave to bear this, and they rose up against him, calling the English to help them. Sir John Moore was sent first, and he marched an army into Spain; but, though the Spaniards were brave, they were not steady, and when Napoleon sent more troops he was obliged to march back over the steep hills, covered with snow, to Corunna, where he had left the ships. The French followed him, and he had to fight a battle to drive them back, that his soldiers might embark in quiet. It was a great victory; but in the midst of it Sir John Moore was wounded by a cannon shot, and only live long enough to hear that the battle was won. He was buried at the dead of night on the ramparts of Corunna, wrapped in his cloak.

However, before the year was over, Sir Arthur Wellesley was sent out to Portugal and Spain. He never once was beaten, and though twice he had had to retreat into Portugal, he soon won back the ground he had lost; and in three years' time he had driven the French quite out of Spain, and even crossed the Pyrenean mountains after them, forcing them back into their own country, and winning the battle of Toulouse on their own ground. This grand war had more victories in it than you will easily remember. The chief of them were at Salamanca, Vittoria, Orthes, and Toulouse; and the whole war was called the Peninsular War, because it was fought in the Peninsular of France and Spain. Sir Arthur Wellesley had been made duke of Wellington, to reward him, and he set off across France to meet the armies of the other European countries. For, while the English were fighting in Spain, the other states of Europe had all joined together against Napoleon, and driven him away from robbing them, and hunted him at last to Paris, where they made him give up all his unlawful power. The right king of France, Louis XVIII., was brought home, and Napoleon was sent to a little island named Elba, in the Mediterranean Sea, where it was thought he could do no harm.

But only the next year he managed to escape, and came back to France, where all his old soldiers were delighted to see him again. The king was obliged to fly, and Napoleon was soon at the head of as large and fierce an army as ever. The first countries that were ready to fight with him were England and Prussia. The Duke of Wellington with the English, and Marshal Blucher with the Prussian army, met him on the field of Waterloo, in Belgium; and there he was so entirely defeated that he had to flee away from the field. But he found no rest or shelter anywhere, and at last was obliged to give himself up to the captain of an English ship named the Bellerophon. He was taken to Plymouth harbor, and kept in the ship while it was being determined what should be done with him: and at length it was decided to send him to St. Helena, a very lonely island far away in the Atlantic Ocean, whence he would have no chance of escaping. There he was kept for five years, at the end of which time he died.

The whole of Europe was at peace again; but the poor old blind King George did not know it, nor how much times had changed in his long reign. The war had waked people up from the dull state they had been in so long, and much was going on that began greater changes than anyone thought of. Sixty years before, when he began to reign, the roads were so bad that it took three days to go by coach to London from Bath; now they were smooth and good, and fine swift horses were kept at short stages, which made the coaches take only a few hours on the journey. Letters came much quicker and more safely; there were a great many newspapers, and everybody was more alive. Some great writers there were, too: the Scottish poet Walter Scott, who wrote some of the most delightful tales there are in the world; and three who lived at the lakes – Wordsworth, Southey, and Coleridge. It was only in this reign that people cared to write books for children. Mrs. Trimmer, and another good lady called Hannah More, were trying to get the poor in the villages better taught; and there was a very good Yorkshire gentleman – William Wilberforce – who was striving to make people better.

As to people's looks in those days, they had left off wigs – except bishops, judges, and lawyers, in their robes. Men had their hair short and curly, and wore coats shaped like evening ones – generally blue, with brass buttons – buff waistcoats, and tight trousers tucked into their boots, tight stocks round their necks, and monstrous shirt- frills. Ladies had their gowns and pelisses made very short-waisted, and as tight and narrow as they could be, though with enormous sleeves in them, and their hair in little curls on their foreheads. Old ladies wore turbans in evening dress; and both they and their daughters had immense bonnets and hats, with a high crown and very large front.

In the 1820, the good old king passed away.

CHAPTER XLVI.

GEORGE IV. A.D. 1820 – 1830.

George IV. was not much under sixty years old when he came to the throne, and had really been king in all but the name for eight years past. He had been married to the Princess Caroline of Brunswick, much against his will, for she was, though a princess, far from being a lady in any of her ways, and he disliked her from the first moment he saw her; and though he could not quite treat her as Henry VIII. had treated Anne of Cleves, the two were so unhappy together that, after the first year, they never lived in the same house. They had had one child, a daughter, named Charlotte – a good, bright, sensible high- spirited girl – on whom all the hopes of the country were fixed; but as she grew up, there were many troubles between her love and her duty towards her father and mother. As soon as the peace was made, the Princess of Wales went to Italy and lived there, with a great many people of bad characters about her. Princess Charlotte was married to Prince Leopold of Saxe-Coburg, and was very happy with him; but, to the great grief of all England, she died in the bloom of her youth, the year before her grandfather.

George IV., though he was much alone in the world, prepared to have a most splendid coronation; but as soon as his wife heard that he was king, she set off to come to England and be crowned with him. He was exceedingly angry, forbade her name to be put into the Prayer-book as queen, and called on the House of Lords to break his marriage with one who had proved herself not worthy to be a wife. There was a great uproar about it, for though the king's friends wanted him to be rid of her, all the country knew that he had been no better to her than she had been to him, and felt it unfair that the weaker one should have all the shame and disgrace, and the stronger one none. One of Caroline's defenders said that if her name were left out of the Litany, yet still she was prayed for there as one who was desolate and oppressed. People took up her cause much more hotly than deserved, and the king was obliged to give up the enquiry into her behavior, but still he would not let her be crowned. In the midst of all the splendor and solemnity in Westminster Abbey, a carriage was driven to the door and entrance was demanded for the queen; but she was kept back, and the people did not seem disposed to interrupt the show by doing anything in her favor, as she and her friends had expected. She went back to her rooms, and, after being more foolish than ever in her ways, died of fretting and pining. It is a sad history, where both were much to blame; and it shows how hateful to the king she must have been, that, when Napoleon died he was told his greatest enemy was dead, and he answered, "When did *she* die?" But if he had been a good man himself, and not selfish, he would have borne with the poor, ill brought up, giddy girl, when first she came, and that would have prevented her going so far astray.

George IV. made two journeys – one to Scotland, and the other to Ireland. He was the first of the House of Brunswick who ever visited these other two kingdoms, and he was received in both with great splendor and rejoicing; but after this his health began to fail, and he disliked showing himself. He spent most of his time at a house he had built for himself at Brighton, called the Pavilion, and at Windsor, where he used to drive about in the park. He was kind and gracious to those with whom he associated, but they were as few as possible.

He was vexed and angry at having to consent to the Bill for letting Roman Catholics sit in Parliament, and hold other office – the same that his father had stood out against. It was not that he cared for one religion more than another, for he had never been a religious man, but he saw that it would be the beginning of a great many changes that would alter the whole state of things. His next brother, Frederick, Duke of York, died before him; and the third, William, Duke of Clarence, who had been brought up as an officer in the navy, was a friend of the Whigs, and of those who were ready to make alterations.

Changes were coming of themselves, though – for inventions were making progress in this time of peace. People had begun to find out the great power of steam, and had made it move the ships, which had hitherto depended upon the winds, and thus it became much easier to travel from one country to another and to send goods. Steam was also being used to work engines for spinning and weaving cotton, linen, and wool, and for working metals; so that what had hitherto been done by hand, by small numbers of skilful people, was now brought about by large machines, where the labor was done by steam; but quantities of people were needed to assist the engine. And as steam cannot be had without fire, and most of the coal is in the Northern parts of England, almost all of these works were set up in them, and people flocked to get work there, so that the towns began to grow very large. Manchester was one, with Liverpool as the sea-port from which to send its calico and get its cotton. Sheffield and Birmingham grew famous for works in iron and steel, and so on; and all this tended to make the manufacturers as rich and great as the old lords and squires, who had held most of the power in England ever since, at the Revolution, they had got it away from the king. Everyone saw that some great change would soon come; but before it came to the point George IV. fell ill, and died after a reign of twenty years in reality, but of only ten in name, the first five of which were spent in war, and the last fifteen in peace. The Duke of Wellington and Sir Robert Peel were his chief ministers – for the duke was as clear-headed in peace as he was in war.

CHAPTER XLVII.

WILLIAM IV. A.D. 1830 – 1837.

George IV. had, as you know, no child living at the time of his death. His next brother, Frederick Duke of York, died before him, likewise without children, so the crown went to William, Duke of Clarence, third son of George III. He had been a sailor in his younger days, but was an elderly man when he came to the throne. He was a dull and not a very wise man, but good-natured and kind, and had an open, friendly, sailor manner; and his wife, Queen Adelaide, of Saxe- Meiningen, was an excellent woman, whom everyone respected. They never had any children but two daughters who died in infancy: and everyone knew that the next heir must be the Princess Victoria, daughter to the next brother, Edward, Duke of Kent, who had died the year after she was born.

King William IV. had always been friendly with the Whigs, who wanted power for the people. Those who went furthest among them were called Radicals, because they wanted a radical reform – that is, going to the root. In fact, it was time to alter the way of sending members to the House of Commons, for some of the towns that had once been big enough to choose one were now deserted and grown very small, while on the other hand, others which used to be little villages, like Birmingham and Brighton, had now become very large, and full of people.

The Duke of Wellington and his friends wanted to consider the best way of setting these things to rights, but the Radicals wanted to do much more and much faster than he was willing to grant. The poor fancied that the new rights proposed would make them better off all at once, and that every man would get a fat pig in his sty and as much bread as he wanted; and they were so angry at any delay, that they went about in bands burning the hay-ricks and stacks of corn, to frighten their landlords. And the Duke of Wellington's great deeds were forgotten in the anger of the mob, who gathered round him, ready to abuse and pelt him as he rode along; and yet, as they saw his quiet, calm way of going on, taking no heed to them, and quite fearless, no one raised a hand. They broke the windows of his house in London, though, and he had iron blinds put up to protect them. He went out of office, and the Whigs came in, and then the Act of Parliament was passed which was called the Reform bill – because it set to rights what had gone wrong as to which towns should have members of their own, and, besides, allowed everyone in a borough town, who rented a house at ten pounds a year, to vote for the member of Parliament. A borough is a town that has a member of Parliament, and a city is one that is large enough to have a mayor and an alderman to manage its affairs at home.

Several more changes were made under King William. Most of the great union workhouses were built then, and it was made less easy to get help from the parish without going to live in one. This was meant to cure people of being idle and liking to live on other folk's money – and it has done good in that way; but workhouses are sad places for the poor aged people who cannot work, and it is a great kindness to help them to keep out of them.

The best thing that was done was the setting the slaves free. Look at the map of America, and you will see a number of islands – beautiful places, where sug-

sugar-canes, and coffee, and spices grow. Many of these belong to the English, but it is too hot for Englishmen to work there. So, for more than a hundred years, there had been a wicked custom that ships should go to Africa, and there the crews would steal negro men, women and children, or buy them of tribes of fierce negroes who had made them captive, and carry them off to the West Indies Islands, where they were sold to work for their masters, just as cattle are bought and sold. An English gentleman – William Wilberforce – worked half his life to get this horrible slave trade forbidden; and at last he succeeded, in the year 1807, whilst George III. was still reigning. But though no more blacks were brought from Africa, still the people in the West Indies were allowed to keep, and buy and sell the slaves they already had. So Wilberforce and his friends still worked on until the time of William IV., when, in 1834, all the slaves in the British dominions were set free.

This reign only lasted seven years, and there were no wars in it; so the only other thing that I have to tell you about it is, that people had gone on from finding that steam could be made to work their ships to making it draw carriages. Railways were being made for trains of carriages and vans to be drawn by one steam engine. The oldest of all was opened in 1830, the very year that William IV. began to reign, and that answered so well that more and more began to be made, and the whole country to be covered with a network of railways, so the people and goods could be carried about much quicker than ever was dreamt of in old times; while steam-ships were made larger and larger, and to go greater distances.

Besides this, many people in England found

there was not work or food enough for them at home, and went to settle in Canada, and Australia, and Van Dieman's Land, and New Zealand, making, in all these distant places, the new English homes called colonies; and thus there have come to be English people wherever the sun shines.

William IV. died in the year 1837. He was the last English king who had the German State of Hanover. It cannot belong to a woman, so it went to his brother Ernest, instead of his niece Victoria.

CHAPTER XLVIII.

VICTORIA. A.D. 1837 – 1855.

The Princess Victoria, daughter of the Duke of Kent, was but eighteen years old when she was Queen of England.

She went with her mother, the Duchess of Kent, to live, sometimes at Buckingham Palace and sometimes at Windsor Castle, and the next year she was crowned in state at Westminster Abbey. Everyone saw then how kind she was, for when one of the lords, who was very old, stumbled on the steps as he came to pay her homage, she sprang up from her throne to help him.

Three years later she was married to Prince Albert of Saxe-Coburg, a most excellent men, who made it his whole business to help her in all her duties as sovereign of the great country, without putting himself forward. Nothing ever has been more beautiful than the way those two behaved to one another; she never forgetting that he was her husband and she only his wife, and he always remembering that she was really the queen, and that he had no power at all. He had a clear head and good judgment that everyone trusted to, and yet he always kept himself in the background, that the queen might have all the credit of whatever was done.

He took much pains to get all that was good and beautiful encouraged, and to turn people's minds to doing things not only in the quickest and cheapest, but in the best and most beautiful way possible. One of these plans that he carried out was to set up what he called an International Exhibition, namely – a great building, to which every country was invited to send specimens of all its arts and manufactures. It was called the World's Fair. The house was of glass, and was a beautiful thing in itself. It was opened on the 1st of May, 1851; and, though there have been many great International Exhibitions since, not one has come up to the first.

People talked as if the World's Fair was to make all nations friends; but it is not showing off their laces and their silks, their ironwork and brass, their pictures and statues, that can keep them at peace; and, only two years after the Great Exhibition, a great war broke out in Europe – only a year after the great Duke of Wellington had died, full of years and honors.

The only country in Europe that is not Christian is Turkey; and the Russians have always greatly wished to conquer Turkey, and join it on to their great empire. The Turks have been getting less powerful for a long time past, and finding it harder to govern the country; and one day the Emperor of Russia asked the English ambassador, Sir Hamilton Seymour, if he did not think the Turkish power a very sick man who would soon be dead. Sir Hamilton Seymour knew what this meant; and he knew the English did not think it right that the Russians should drive out the Sultan of Turkey – even though he is not a Christian; so he made the emperor understand that if the sick man did die, it would not be for want of doctors.

Neither the English nor the French could bear that the Russians should get so much power as they would have, if they gained all the countries down to the Mediterranean Sea; so, as soon as ever the Russians began to attack the Turks, the English and French armies were sent to defend them; and they found the best way of doing this was to go and fight the Russians in their own country, namely – the Crimea, the peninsula which hangs as it were, down into the Black Sea. So, in the autumn of the year 1854, the English and French armies, under Lord Raglan and Marshal St. Arnaud, were landed in the Crimea, where they gained a great victory on their first landing, called the battle of the Alma, and then besieged the city of Sebastopol. It was a very long siege, and in the course of it the two armies suffered sadly from the cold and damp, and there was much illness; but a brave English Lady, named Florence Nightingale, went out with a number of nurses to take care of the sick and wounded, and thus she saved a great many lives. There were two more famous battles. One was when six hundred English horsemen were sent by mistake against a whole battery of Russian cannon, and rode on as bravely as if they were not seeing their comrades shot down, till scarcely half were left. This was called the Charge of Balaklava. The other battle was when the Russians crept out, late in the evening of November 5, to attack the English camp: and there was a dreadful fight by night and in the early morning on the heights of Inkerman; but at last the English won the battle, and gave the day a better honor that it had had before. Then came a terrible winter of watching the city and firing at the walls; and when at last, on the 18th of June, 1855, it was assaulted, the defenders beat the attack off; and Lord Raglan, worn out with care and vexation, died a few days after. However, soon another attack was made, and in September half the city was won. The Emperor of Russia had died during the war, and his son made peace, on condition that Sebastopol should not be fortified again, and that the Russians should let the Turks alone, and keep no fleet in the Black Sea.

In this war news flew faster than ever it had done before. You heard how Benjamin Franklin found that electricity – that strange power of which lightning is the visible sign – could be carried along upon metal wire. It has since been made out how to make the touch of a magnet at one end of these wires make the other end move so that letters can be pointed to, words spelt out and messages sent to any distance with really the speed of lightning. This is the wonderful electric telegraph, of which you see the wires upon the railway.

CHAPTER XLIX.

VICTORIA. A.D. 1857 – 1860.

Peace had been made after the Crimean war, and everybody hoped it was going to last, when very sad news came from India. You know I told you the English people had gone to live in India, and had gradually gained more and more lands there, so that they were making themselves rulers and governors over all that great country. They had some of the regiments of the English army to help them to keep up their power, and a great many soldiers besides – Hindoos, or natives of India, who had English officers, and were taught to fight in the English manner. These Hindoo soldiers were called Sepoys. They were not Christians, but were some of them Mahommedans, and some believed in the strange religion of India, which teached people to believe in a great many gods – some of them very savage and cruel ones, according to their stories, and which forbids them many very simple things. One of the things it forbids is the killing a cow, or touching beef, or any part of it.

Now, it seems the Sepoys had grown discontented with the English; and, besides that, there came out a new sort of cartridge – that is, little parcels of powder and shot with which to load fire-arms. The Sepoys took it into their heads that these cartridges had grease in them taken from cows, and that it was a trick on the part of the English to make them break the rules of their religion, and force them to become Christians. In their anger they made a conspiracy together; and, in many of the places in India, they then suddenly turned upon their English officers, and shot them down on their parade ground, and then they went to the houses and killed every white woman and child they could meet with. Some few had very wonderful escapes, and were treated kindly by native friends; and many showed great bravery and piety in their troubles. After that the Sepoys marched away to the city of Delhi, where an old man lived who had once been king, and they set him up to be king, while every English person left in the city was murdered.

The English regiments in India made haste to come into Bengal, to try to save their country-folk who had shut themselves up in the towns or strong places, and were being besieged there by the Sepoys. A great many were in barracks in Cawnpore. It was not a strong place, and only had a mud wall round; but there was a native prince called the Nana Sahib, who had always seemed a friend to the officers – had gone out hunting with them, and invited them to his house. They thought themselves safe near him; but, to their horror, he forgot all this, and joined the Sepoys. The cannon were turned against them, and the Sepoys watched all day the barrack yard where they were shut in, and shot everyone who went for water. At last, after more pain and misery than we can bear to think of, they gave themselves up to the Nana, and horrible to tell, he killed them all. The men were shot the first day, and the women and little children were then shut up in a house, where they were kept for a night. Then the Nana heard that the English army was coming, and in his fright and rage he sent in his men, who killed everyone of them, and threw their bodies into a deep well. The English came up the next day, and were nearly mad with grief and anger. They could not lay hands on the Nana, but they punished all the people he employed; and they were so furious that they hardly showed any mercy to another Sepoy after that dreadful sight.

There were some more English holding out in the city of Lucknow, and they longed to go to their relief; but first Delhi, where the old king was, had to be taken; and, as it was a very strong place, it was a long time before it was conquered; but at last the gates of the city were blown up by three brave men, and the whole army made their way in. More troops had been sent out from England to help their comrades, and they were able at last to march to Lucknow. There, week after week, the English soldiers, men of business, ladies, soldier's wives, and little children, had bravely waited, with the enemy round, and shot so often coming through the buildings that they had chiefly to live in the cellars; and the food was so scanty and bad, that the sickly people and the little babies mostly died; and no one seemed able to get well if once he was wounded. Help came at last. The brave Sir Colin Campbell, who had been sent out from home, brought the army to their rescue, and they were saved. The Sepoys were beaten in every fight; and at last the terrible time of the mutiny was over, and India quiet again.

In 1860, the queen and all the nation had a grievous loss in the death of the good Prince Consort, Albert, who died of a fever at Windsor Castle, and was mourned for by everyone, as if he had been a relation or friend. He left nine children, of whom the eldest, Victoria, the Princess Royal, was married to the Prince of Prussia. He had done everything to help forward improvements; and the country only found out how wise and good he was after he was taken away.

Pains began to be taken to make the great towns

healthier. It is true that the plague has never come to England since the reign of Charles II., but those sad diseases, cholera and typhus fever, come where people will not attend to cleanliness. The first time the cholera came was in the year 1833, under William IV.; and that was the last time of all, because it was a new disease, and the doctors did not know what to do to cure it. But now they understand it much better – both how to treat, and, what is better, how to keep it away; and that is by keeping everything sweet and clean.

CHAPTER L.

VICTORIA. A.D. 1860 – 1872.

One more chapter, which, however, does not finish the history of good Queen Victoria, and these Stories of the History of England will be over.

All the nation rejoiced very much when the queen's eldest son, Albert Edward, the Prince of Wales, married Alexandra, daughter to the king of Denmark. Her father and mother brought her to England, and the prince met her on board ship in the mouth of the Thames; and there was a most beautiful and joyous procession through London. When they were married the next day, in St. George's Chapel at Windsor, the whole of England made merry, and there were bonfires on every hill, and illuminations in every town, so that the whole island was glowing with brightness all that Spring evening.

There is a country in Abyssinia, south of Egypt. The people there are Christians, but they have had very little to do with other nations, and have grown very dull and half savage; indeed they have many horrid and disgusting customs, and have forgotten all the teaching that would have made them better. Of late years there had been some attempt to wake them up and teach them; and they had a clever king named Theodore, who seemed pleased and willing to improve himself and his nation. He allowed missionaries to come and try to teach his people what Christianity means a little better than they knew before, and invited skilled workmen to come and teach his people. They came; but not long after Theodore was affronted by the English Government, and shut them all up in prison. Messages were sent to insist upon his releasing them, but he did not attend or understand; and at last an army was sent to land on the coast from the east, under General Napier, and march to his capital, which was called Magdala, and stood on a hill.

General Napier managed so well that there was no fighting on the road. He came to the gates of Magdala, and threatened to fire upon it if the prisoners were not given up to him. He waited till the time was up, and then caused his troops to begin the attack. The Abyssinians fled away, and close by one of the gates Theodore was found lying dead, shot through. No one is quite sure whether one of his servants killed him treacherously, or whether he killed himself in his rage and despair. England did not try to keep Abyssinia though it was conquered; but it was left to the royal family whom Theodore had turned out, and Theodore's little son, about five years old, was brought to England; but, as he could not bear the cold winter, he was sent to a school in India.

This, which was in the year 1868, was the last war the English have had. There has been fighting all round and about in Europe, especially a great war between France and Prussia in 1870; but the only thing the English had to do with that, was the sending out of doctors and nurses, with all the good things for sick people that could be thought of, to take care of all the poor wounded on both sides, and lessen their suffering as much as possible. They all wore red crosses on their sleeves, and put up a red-cross flag over the houses where they were taking care of the sick and wounded, and then no one on either side fired upon them.

An Act of Parliament has given the right to vote, at the election of the House of Commons, to much poorer men than used to have it. It is to be hoped that they will learn to use wisely this power of helping to choose those who make the laws and govern the country. To give them a better chance of doing so, a law has been made that no child shall be allowed to grow up without any teaching at all, but that those who are too poor to pay for their own schooling shall be paid for by the State, and that their parents shall be obliged to send them. The great thing is to learn to know and do one's duty. If one only learns to be clever with one's head, without trying to be good at the same time, it is of very little use. But I hope you will try to mind your duty – first to God and then to man; and if you do that, God will prosper you and bless you.

www.ingramcontent.com/pod-product-compliance
Lightning Source LLC
Chambersburg PA
CBHW021949290426
44108CB00012B/995